What If We Succeed?

Unseen Struggles, Leadership Failures, and Triumphs in America's Community Colleges and Among Their Students

Douglas B Sims, PhD

What If We Succeed?

Douglas B Sims

What If We Succeed?

Foreword

I am the Dean of a large community college's School of Science, Engineering, and Mathematics. During the Spring term of 2024, I vividly remember a fellow dean's reaction when the Provost suggested expanding the seat count in general education courses to help students earn their degrees faster. With genuine terror in his eyes, he replied, "What if we succeed?" You'd think he'd seen a ghost, but no, he was worried that doing something right might lead to success and, heaven forbid, his own accountability. Was he concerned that students would graduate, we'd have to hire more faculty, or that expanding the seats would bring accountability to the forefront of leadership and staff?

That's when it hit me—right in the middle of our weekly three-hour meeting: the fear of success is like a bad horror movie plot driving the lack of achievement at America's community colleges. It turns out our biggest nightmare isn't budget cuts or accreditation woes—it's accidentally doing our jobs too well! This meeting led me to write this book on America's unsung heroes of higher education: the community colleges.

The formation and growth of American community colleges represent a transformative chapter in U.S. higher education. Established in the early 20th century to provide accessible, affordable, and flexible education, these institutions aimed to bridge the gap between high school and university education. They catered to students needing an intermediate step before entering four-year institutions or preparing for the workforce. The flexibility and inclusivity of community colleges allowed them to serve non-traditional students, including adult learners, part-time students, and those seeking vocational training or career changes. Over the decades, community colleges have significantly evolved to meet the changing educational, economic, and social needs of the nation.

Despite their positive impact and evolution, community colleges face significant challenges that hinder their effectiveness. One primary issue is the inconsistent transfer of credits to universities, where not all credits earned at community colleges are accepted by four-year institutions, leading to wasted time and resources for students. The complexity and variability of articulation agreements can further confuse and frustrate students. Additionally, the perception of the lack of academic rigor at the two-year institutions results in lower transfer success rates and higher dropout rates. Resource constraints also pose a major problem, as limited funding affects the quality of education and student services. Inadequate support services, such as academic advising, career counseling, semantically poor leadership, and transfer support, can hinder student success. Furthermore, disparities in access and outcomes based on socioeconomic status, race, and geographic location continue to persist. Many students face additional challenges, such as balancing work, family responsibilities, and education, requiring more comprehensive support systems. By addressing these challenges through streamlined credit transfers, enhanced academic support, improved funding, and expanded student services, community colleges can better serve their students and fulfill their evolving role in the higher education landscape.

Acknowledgments

I would like to express my genuine gratitude to my wife for her resolute support, guidance, and the remarkable journey of love and marriage we've shared for over 34 years. Your presence has been my anchor and inspiration throughout life and our journey.

I am also profoundly grateful to our two children, who have enriched our lives and taught us the joys and challenges of parenting. Watching you grow and experience life has been a constant source of pride and learning.

I extend my heartfelt thanks to my friends and colleagues. Observing your lives, receiving your input, and sharing insights with you have greatly contributed to this book. Your contributions have been wonderful and indispensable, and I am grateful for your role in this endeavor. Sharing our lives with you and having you share your lives with us added depth and real-world perspectives to this work. Your openness and experience have been invaluable.

What If We Succeed?

Table of Contents

Foreword v

Acknowledgments vii

1. Catalysts of Community College Success....................................... 1

2. Blueprints of Community College Governance........................... 26

3. Financial Aid abuse by Higher Education 34

4. Guiding Success: Leadership in Community Colleges............... 43

5. Beyond Grades: Holistic Student Success 56

6. Facing Forward: Challenges and Opportunities for Com. Colleges 71

7. Overcoming the Odds: Tackling Com. College Student Challenges..... 80

8. Charting the Future: Community College Trends and Predictions 84

9. Cornerstones of Opportunity: Critical Role in Higher Education....... 101

10. Path Forward: Overcoming Challenges, Embracing Opportunities ...108

11. Embracing the Future: Embracing Community College Evolution....111

Bibliography 115

About the Author.. 127

Chapter 1

Catalysts of Community College Success

T he true unsung heroes of higher education are community colleges. They offer accessible, affordable, and flexible educational opportunities to millions of students, often while wearing metaphorical capes (but sadly, no actual spandex suits). But never have I ever heard a senior manager say, "What if we succeed?" in response to the head of a division, with sheer terror in their eyes—like they'd just seen a ghost holding a performance review. As these institutions evolve to offer bachelor's degrees, they're not just meeting local workforce needs—they're creating superhero pathways for non-traditional students to achieve their academic and career aspirations.

"Education is the most powerful weapon which you can use to change the world" ~Nelson Mandela

Community colleges are at the forefront of a transformative era in higher education, tasked with providing accessible, affordable, and flexible education to a diverse population, making failure not an option. By prioritizing student success and institutional effectiveness through strategic improvements in support services, resource allocation, and leadership development, they will continue to be vital contributors to the educational and economic well-being of their communities and the nation.

This book dives into the pivotal role of community colleges in serving diverse student populations, including first-generation college students and those from low-income backgrounds. Despite facing villains like transferability issues, leadership challenges, and funding constraints, community colleges remain committed to their mission of fostering academic achievement and personal growth.

We'll explore innovative solutions like enhanced financial support, improved articulation agreements, and comprehensive support services, showing how community colleges can continue to thrive (cue the triumphant theme music). Drawing inspiration from successful education systems, we'll examine how equity and inclusion can further enhance the mission of these vital institutions.

"People look at me like I'm crazy when I say that our greatest partnership here at Ohio State should be with the community colleges" ~Gordon Gee

Join us as we uncover the strategies, successes, and occasional hilarious failures that position community colleges as essential contributors to the educational and economic well-being of their communities and the nation. Get ready for a journey filled with inspiration, innovation, and maybe a few cape-wearing educators along the way.

Community colleges have undergone significant transformations over the past few decades, shifting their primary focus from facilitating immediate employment to becoming transfer platforms for students aiming to continue their education at four-year institutions. Initially, community colleges were heavily focused on providing vocational training and associate degrees that prepared students for immediate entry into the workforce. These programs were designed to meet the needs of local industries and businesses, offering a skilled workforce for specific trades, and played a crucial role in local workforce development by offering short-term certificate programs and associate degrees in fields like nursing, automotive repair, and welding (Kane & Rouse, 1999).

Today, community colleges have expanded their focus beyond vocational training and associate degrees to include transfer pathways to four-year institutions, comprehensive support services, opportunities for lifelong learning, and their own workforce-connected bachelor's degrees. This shift is driven by the increasing demand for higher education accessibility, the evolving needs of the modern workforce, and the recognition of the importance of providing flexible educational opportunities for a diverse student population.

"Don't let what you cannot do interfere with what you can do."
~John Wooden

Over the years, community colleges developed robust transfer agreements with four-year institutions, allowing students to complete the first two years of their bachelor's degree at a community college before transferring to a university. To facilitate this shift, community colleges expanded their curriculum to include more general education courses that align with the requirements of four-year institutions. The affordability of community colleges made higher education more accessible to a broader population, including non-traditional students, part-time students, and those from lower-income backgrounds (Cohen, Brawer, & Kisker, 2013).

Universities, however, often do not accept community college transfer credits due to financial incentives, as retaining students for a full four-year course maximizes their tuition revenue. Additionally, universities seek to maintain control over their curricula to ensure academic standards and uphold their competitive status in the higher education market. Moreover, universities weaponize rigor and quality by stating the quality of community college courses as "not as rigorous or of high quality " compared to university offerings, which further justifies their reluctance to accept transfer credits.

Contrary to the perception that community college courses lack rigor and quality, numerous studies and reports have demonstrated that these institutions provide robust academic programs that adequately prepare students for university-level coursework. Research from the Pathways to College Network highlights that community colleges maintain rigorous standards and hold accreditations from the same bodies that oversee four-year universities, ensuring comparable quality in education (Higher Education, 2006; Quality Matters, 2019). Additionally, articulation agreements between community colleges and universities are increasingly common, designed to facilitate seamless credit transfers and uphold academic continuity. These agreements highlight the collaborative effort to recognize the value of community college education and support student success in transitioning to higher education (AdLit, n.d.; Higher Education, 2006).

Despite these positive changes, there are several challenges associated with the transfer model. A significant challenge is the inconsistent transfer of credits, with many four-year institutions not accepting all credits earned at community colleges. This results in students losing valuable time and resources (Monaghan & Attewell,

2015). The complexity and variability of articulation agreements between community colleges and four-year institutions can confuse and frustrate students (Handel, 2013). Additionally, some community college students may not be adequately prepared for the academic rigor of four-year institutions, resulting in lower transfer success rates and higher dropout rates (Jenkins & Fink, 2015). Many students enter community colleges needing remedial education, which can delay their progress and increase their educational costs (Bailey, Jeong, & Cho, 2010).

Resource constraints are another significant issue. Community colleges often operate with limited funding, impacting the quality of education and student services they can provide (Dougherty & Townsend, 2006). Inadequate support services, such as academic advising, career counseling, and transfer support, can hinder student success (Karp, 2011). Furthermore, while community colleges aim to provide accessible education, there are still disparities in access and outcomes based on socioeconomic status, race, and geographic location (Ma & Baum, 2016). Many community college students face additional challenges, such as balancing work, family responsibilities, and education, which require more comprehensive support systems (Goldrick-Rab, 2010).

Thirty years ago, my journey through community college felt like trying to navigate a maze with a blindfold on—and no one handed me a map. Academic advising? More like academic guessing. Career counseling? I think I got more advice from my grandma about becoming a professional bingo player. And as for transfer support, let's just say I might have had better luck using smoke signals to communicate with four-year institutions.

Despite community colleges' noble mission of providing accessible education, I quickly discovered that access was about as reliable as my old dial-up internet—painfully slow and full of disconnects. Coming from a low-income background, I was already balancing work, family responsibilities, and education like a circus act on a unicycle. Without comprehensive support systems, it was like they handed me that unicycle but forgot the training wheels.

Looking back, it's a wonder I made it through, and I can't help but laugh at the absurdity of it all. I may have lacked guidance, but at least I gained a pretty good sense of humor along the way!

To address these challenges, several areas for improvement should be considered. Streamlining credit transfers by developing standardized transfer processes and improving articulation agreements can ensure that more credits are transferable and applicable to bachelor's degree programs (Gandara, Alvarado, Driscoll, & Orfield, 2012). Enhancing academic support through tutoring, mentoring, and preparatory courses can help students transition successfully to four-year institutions (Karp, 2011). Improving funding for community colleges can enhance educational quality, faculty resources, and student services (Dougherty & Townsend, 2006). Expanding support services to address the diverse needs of community college students, including mental health resources, childcare, and financial advising, is also crucial (Ma & Baum, 2016). Strengthening partnerships between community colleges, four-year institutions, and local industries can create more seamless pathways for students and ensure alignment with workforce needs (Gandara et al., 2012). By addressing these challenges and focusing on continuous improvement, community colleges can better serve their students and fulfill their evolving role in the higher education landscape.

As someone who's tried to navigate the parallel universes of academia and industry, I've often felt like I was living in two different centuries. In academia, it was like we were still using floppy disks and asking students to learn skills that were cutting-edge... in the 90s. Meanwhile, industry was out there flying around in self-driving cars and talking about things that sounded like science fiction.

The truth is, strengthening partnerships between community colleges, four-year institutions, and local industries is like getting these two worlds to finally have a conversation—and not just awkward small talk, but a real, meaningful dialogue. If we could get academia to stop dusting off textbooks from the Stone Age and start aligning with what's actually happening in the workforce, students wouldn't just graduate with a degree; they'd graduate with a real shot at landing a job. It's high time we built a bridge between these worlds, so students don't feel like they're stepping out of a time machine when they enter the workforce!

"A person who never made a mistake never tried anything new."
~Albert Einstein

Community colleges provide accessible, affordable, and flexible educational opportunities to a diverse population of students, including recent high school graduates, working adults, and non-traditional learners. This inclusivity helps to democratize higher education, making it possible for individuals from various socioeconomic backgrounds to pursue postsecondary education and improve their life circumstances. Their importance can be highlighted through several key aspects:

Accessibility and Affordability

One of the primary advantages of community colleges is their accessibility and affordability. With lower tuition rates compared to four-year universities, community colleges make higher education attainable for students who might otherwise be unable to afford it. This affordability is particularly important for low-income students and those who are the first in their families to attend college (Bailey et al., 2015). By providing financial aid, scholarships, and flexible payment plans, community colleges help reduce the financial barriers to education. Community colleges are often geographically dispersed, with campuses located in urban, suburban, and rural areas, making it easier for students to attend classes close to home. This local presence reduces commuting time and costs, further enhancing accessibility. The flexible scheduling options, including evening, weekend, and online classes, accommodate students who may have work, family, or other commitments, allowing them to balance their responsibilities while pursuing their education (Bailey et al., 2015).

Workforce Development

Workforce development programs are designed to provide students with the skills and knowledge required for immediate employment in high-demand fields such as healthcare, information technology, manufacturing, and skilled trades. By partnering with local businesses and industry leaders, community colleges ensure that their curricula are relevant and up to date, meeting the evolving needs of the job market. The impact of community colleges on the economy is significant. By preparing a skilled workforce, these institutions contribute to the economic development of their communities. Graduates of community college programs often find employment in their local areas, thereby supporting local businesses and industries. Furthermore, community colleges offer customized training programs for incumbent workers, helping businesses to upskill their employees and remain competitive. This symbiotic relationship between community colleges and local economies fosters economic growth and stability (Jones, 2019).

From my experience, partnering with local businesses and industry leaders was like finally getting the inside scoop on what the cool kids were doing. Instead of guessing what skills might be useful in the job market (like trying to predict the weather in a hurricane), we actually got the real deal from the people who knew best. This meant our curricula weren't just relevant—they were cutting-edge, like trading in a typewriter for the latest smartphone.

By working together, we made sure our students were learning skills that employers needed right now, not just what was trendy back when pagers were the height of technology. It was like giving our graduates a secret weapon—they didn't just step out of college with a degree; they stepped out with a toolkit that made them the Swiss Army knives of the workforce. Trust me, nothing beats the feeling of knowing our students were not just prepared for the job market—they were practically handpicked by it!

Flexibility and Support for Non-Traditional Students

Community colleges are known for their flexibility, catering to non-traditional students, including working adults, part-time students, and those with family responsibilities. They offer a variety of class schedules, online courses, and support services designed to accommodate the unique needs of these students, making it possible for more individuals to pursue higher education (Smith, 2020).

Transfer Rates and Graduation Outcomes for Community College Students

Many community colleges have established transfer agreements with four-year institutions, providing a seamless pathway for students to continue their education (Table below). This system allows students to complete the first two years of their bachelor's degree at a community college before transferring to a university, saving on tuition costs and easing the transition to higher education (Karp, 2012).

Ah, the promise of transfer agreements—a seamless, money-saving path from community college to a four-year university. Sounds like a dream, right? Well, let me tell you, it's more like chasing a mirage in the desert. These agreements start off looking like a golden ticket to success, but before you know it, they're outdated or completely ignored thanks to the good ol' "lack of communication" between schools.

Picture this: you've aced your courses, ready to transfer, only to find out your credits are about as useful as a chocolate teapot. Why? Because somewhere along the line, the schools forgot to update their agreement, and now you're left with a handful of credits that don't transfer. Cue the frustration, extra semesters, and let's not forget—massive student loans that you'll be paying off until you're old enough to use your degree as a coaster in the retirement home.

So, before you get caught in the transfer agreement trap, do your homework, ask all the questions, and make sure your "seamless path" doesn't turn into a never-ending detour. Your future self will thank you!

Studies show however, that 87% of community college students do not earn a bachelor's degree after 6 years upon transferring to a university (Donadel, 2023); a qualification needed in most technical, professional, and office jobs today. The table below provides key metrics for community college students across various states in the United States, focusing on transfer rates and graduation rates after transferring to universities. The transfer rate represents the percentage of community college students who move on to universities, while the graduation rate after transfer indicates the percentage of these transfer students who complete their university degrees (Bailey, Jaggars, & Jenkins, 2015). The table below also shows the percentage of community college students who earn a bachelor's degree once they transfer to the university after 4 years.

"Procrastination makes easy things hard and hard things harder."
~Mason Cooley

For instance, in California, 25% of community college students transfer to universities, and of those, 65% graduate leaving a success rate of 16.25%. This pattern is consistent across other states as well. In Texas, 22.5% of community college students transfer to universities, with a 63.5% graduation rate among those transfers leaving a success rate of 14.29%. Florida sees a 23.8% transfer rate and a 64.2% graduation rate for transfer students leaving a success rate of 15.23%. Similarly, New York has a transfer rate of 24.5%, with 66% of those students graduating from universities leaving a success rate of 16.17% (Bailey, Jaggars, & Jenkins, 2015).

Other states have a similar issue where community college students do not complete a university degree. For instance, Illinois, Pennsylvania, Ohio, Georgia, North Carolina, Michigan, and Nevada show similar trends. Illinois has a 21.7% transfer rate with a 62.8% graduation rate after transfer, while Pennsylvania has a 20.9% transfer rate and a 61.5% graduation rate. Ohio's transfer rate is 22%, with

62.7% of those students graduating. Georgia shows a 23% transfer rate and a 63.8% graduation rate, and North Carolina has a 24% transfer rate with a 64.5% graduation rate. Michigan's transfer rate is 21.3%, with 61% graduating after transfer, and Nevada has a 22.7% transfer rate with a 62.5% graduation rate (Bailey, Jaggars, & Jenkins, 2015). So, the question is, are community colleges making a difference in the lives of students?

These students often face challenges such as financial difficulties, academic struggles, and personal responsibilities, which can impede their ability to finish their education. Many leave with significant debt and without the enhanced job prospects that a degree would provide, making it harder for them to repay their loans (Goldrick-Rab, 2016). This underscores the need for additional support systems, such as academic advising, financial aid, and mental health services, to help transfer students navigate and overcome these challenges, improving their chances of graduating (Selingo, 2016; Kuh, Kinzie, Schuh, & Whitt, 2010).

Students who complete a bachelor's degree after transferring to universities

State	Transfer Rate (%)	Graduation Rate After Transfer (%)	Graduation (%) of Community College students with a BA/BS
California	25	65	16.3
Texas	22.5	63.5	14.3
Florida	23.8	64.2	15.3
New York	24.5	66	16.2
Illinois	21.7	62.8	13.6
Pennsylvania	20.9	61.5	12.9
Ohio	22	62.7	13.8
Georgia	23	63.8	14.7
N. Carolina	24	64.5	15.5
Michigan	21.3	61	13
Nevada	22.7	62.5	14.2

Other challenges community college students face is inadequate academic advising and support services that can leave students ill-prepared for the transition to a four-year institution. Many students do not receive sufficient guidance on navigating the transfer process or understanding the requirements for their intended majors, leading to missed opportunities and extended time in community college (Barshay, 2020; Donadel, 2023). Overall, students who transfer to universities do not complete their degrees, highlighting the importance of targeted support and intervention strategies to aid these students in achieving their educational goals (Bailey et al., 2015; Soares, 2013). These challenges highlight the need for improved financial education, streamlined transfer agreements, and better academic support to help community college students achieve their goal of earning a bachelor's degree.

Promoting Equity and Inclusion

Community colleges also play a significant role in promoting equity and inclusion in higher education. They serve a diverse student population, including underrepresented minorities, first-generation college students, and low-income individuals. By offering accessible education and support services, community colleges help to close the achievement gap and foster a more inclusive society (Santiago, 2018). This is promoted through their open admissions policies, ensuring that higher education is accessible to all, regardless of academic background or financial means. These institutions provide an affordable alternative to traditional four-year universities, significantly reducing the financial burden on students and their families. Additionally, community colleges offer flexible scheduling options, including evening, weekend, and online classes, to accommodate working students and those with family responsibilities.

"You don't have to be great to start, but you have to start to be great."
~ Zig Ziglar

Open admissions policies aim to provide greater access to higher education by allowing any student with a high school diploma or GED to enroll. However, this inclusivity can hurt ill-prepared students by enrolling them in an environment for which they may not be academically ready (Grove, 2023). These students often require substantial remedial courses to catch up, which do not count towards their degrees, prolonging their education and increasing costs (Grove, 2023). To address this, new corequisite courses in math and English have been introduced as a bridge to help students succeed, allowing them to simultaneously take remedial and college-level courses with additional support.

Corequisite courses in math and English help student success by allowing students to enroll in college-level courses while simultaneously receiving the support they need to address gaps in their skills (Bailey et al., 2010; Ran and Lin, 2019). Unlike traditional remedial courses, which students must complete before advancing, corequisite models integrate additional instructional time and support into college-level coursework (Bailey et al., 2010; Ran and Lin, 2019). This approach helps students progress more quickly toward their degrees, improves pass rates in gateway courses (e.g. English and Math), and enhances retention and graduation rates by providing immediate, relevant, and contextualized academic support. Of course, this is one piece of the overall puzzle to success for the modern community college student.

"The expert in anything was once a beginner." ~*Helen Hayes*

Support services are a critical component of community colleges' commitment to equity and inclusion. These services often include academic advising, tutoring, mentoring, and career counseling, all designed to help students navigate the challenges of higher education and achieve their academic and career goals. Moreover, many community colleges have programs specifically targeted at assisting underrepresented groups, such as initiatives to support minority students, veterans, and individuals with disabilities.

Community colleges also play a crucial role in workforce development, providing training and education that aligns with local labor market needs. This not only helps students gain the skills required for employment but also supports economic development in the community. By partnering with local businesses and industries, community colleges can offer programs that lead directly to job opportunities, thereby enhancing social mobility and economic stability for their graduates. Furthermore, community colleges often serve as a gateway for students who aspire to continue their education at four-year institutions. Through articulation agreements and transfer programs, these colleges provide a seamless pathway for students to earn bachelor's degrees, making higher education more attainable for those who might not have considered it otherwise.

Community colleges are vital in promoting equity and inclusion in higher education. By providing accessible, affordable, and flexible educational opportunities, along with comprehensive support services, they help bridge the gap for underrepresented and disadvantaged students. This commitment to serving a diverse student body not only enhances individual lives but also contributes to a more inclusive and equitable society.

Lifelong Learning and Continuing Education

Community colleges are also centers for lifelong learning and continuing education, offering a range of courses for personal enrichment, professional development, and skill enhancement. These programs cater to individuals at various stages of their careers and lives, emphasizing the importance of continuous learning in an ever-changing world (American Association of Community Colleges, 2021). Community colleges are integral to the American education landscape, providing critical opportunities for education, workforce development, and social mobility. Their commitment to accessibility, flexibility, and inclusivity ensures that higher education remains within reach for millions of Americans, supporting both individual aspirations and the broader goals of society.

"There are no shortcuts to any place worth going." ~Beverly Stills

While community colleges promote lifelong learning and continuing education, students need to be aware of several drawbacks to holding only an associate degree or certificate. Limited career advancement is one significant issue, as while an associate degree can provide access to entry-level positions, advancing to higher-level roles often requires a bachelor's degree or more advanced qualifications (College Values Online, 2024). Additionally, individuals with an associate degree tend to earn less over their lifetime compared to those with a bachelor's degree. Although an associate degree offers higher earnings than just a high school diploma, the financial benefits are typically greater with a higher degree (Career Center Penn West, 2024). Furthermore, some industries require advanced knowledge and skills that an associate degree may not fully provide. In fields such as technology, healthcare, and finance, higher degrees might be necessary to stay current with evolving standards and practices (College Values Online, 2024).

History of American Community Colleges

The history of American community colleges spans over a century, reflecting the evolution of higher education in response to societal needs. The concept of junior colleges began to take shape in the early 1900s, with Joliet Junior College, established in 1901 in Illinois, recognized as the first public community college (Cohen & Brawer, 2008; U.S. Department of Education, 1965). Founded by William Rainey Harper, the president of the University of Chicago, and his colleague J. Stanley Brown, they envisioned a two-year institution serving as a bridge between high school and a four-year college (Levinson, 2005; Thelin, 2011; Dougherty, 1994). The movement expanded in 1907 with other junior colleges focusing on liberal arts education and preparation for transfer to four-year institutions.

The 1920s saw a growth in the number of junior colleges, supported by the American Association of Junior Colleges (AAJC), founded in 1920, with a primary focus on providing the first two years of a bachelor's degree (U.S. Department of Education, 2020; American Council on Education, 1947). The Great Depression and World War II in the 1930s and 1940s influenced the mission of junior colleges, increasing emphasis on vocational training and workforce development to meet the economic and industrial needs of the nation (U.S. Department of Education, 2020). The post-World War II era in the 1950s marked a surge in college enrollments due to the GI Bill, with community colleges playing a critical role in accommodating veterans seeking education and training (Brint & Karabel, 1989; Beach, 2011; Vaughan, 1985, 2006). The 1960s marked significant expansion and transformation, with the Higher Education Act of 1965 and other federal and state initiatives increasing funding and support for community colleges, leading to rapid growth and a broadened mission that included adult education, remedial education, and community services (Shaw et al., 1999; Townsend & Bragg, 2006; Bailey et al., 2015).

During the 1970s and 1980s, community colleges continued to expand their role in providing accessible education and training, becoming key players in workforce development and offering programs in response to local labor market needs (Bailey et al., 2015; Brint & Karabel, 1989, 2006; Shaw et al., 1999; Townsend & Bragg, 2006). The open admissions policy became a hallmark, emphasizing access and inclusivity. In the 1990s and 2000s, community colleges increasingly embraced technology, online education, and partnerships with industries, focusing on non-traditional students, including working adults and part-time learners (Beach, 2011; Vaughan, 1985, 2006; Bailey et al., 2015).

In the modern era, from the 2010s to the present, the role of community colleges remains vital in higher education, seen as essential in promoting equity, affordability, and access (Bailey et al., 2015).

Initiatives such as free community college programs, dual enrollment, and pathways to four-year institutions highlight their ongoing importance (Goldrick-Rab, 2016; Bailey et al., 2015; Kahlenberg, 2015). Key characteristics of community colleges include accessibility, affordability, diversity, a local focus, and comprehensive education, offering a variety of programs including transfer degrees, vocational training, continuing education, and remedial education (Goldrick-Rab, 2016; Bailey et al., 2015; Kahlenberg, 2015). The history of community colleges in the United States reflects their adaptive and responsive nature, continually evolving to meet the educational and economic needs of society. They play a critical role in providing opportunities for lifelong learning and contributing to the development of a skilled workforce.

Community college students face a unique set of challenges compared to their peers at four-year universities. Financial constraints are a significant issue, as many students struggle with the costs of tuition, books, supplies, transportation, and living expenses, often with less access to financial aid. Academically, many community college students are underprepared for college-level coursework and may require remedial classes, and they often have fewer academic advising and mentorship resources. Balancing responsibilities is another major challenge, as many community college students are non-traditional, juggling work, family, and school obligations, which can strain their time and energy. The transfer process to four-year institutions can be complex and uncertain, with credits not always transferring seamlessly and lacking comprehensive articulation agreements.

Community colleges often have fewer institutional resources, such as state-of-the-art facilities, research opportunities, and technology, as well as fewer extracurricular activities and clubs, impacting students' personal and professional development. Social integration and campus engagement are also limited, with fewer opportunities to build strong peer networks. Community colleges typically have lower graduation and retention rates, influenced by the myriad challenges their students face and the often less robust support systems than universities. A stigma can also be associated with attending a community college, affecting students' self-esteem and motivation, as well as their transfer and job prospects. Lastly, community colleges serve a more diverse population, including older and part-time students, which brings a range of needs and challenges that may not be as prevalent at four-year universities. These challenges underscore the need for tailored support systems and policies to help community college students succeed and achieve their educational goals.

"I think it's possible for ordinary people to choose to be extraordinary."
~*Elon Musk*

Community colleges often get a bad rap, unfairly labeled as the last resort for students who are considered lower-tier or as having no real future. This perception is fueled by stereotypes and, unfortunately, reinforced by pop culture. Shows like "Are You Smarter Than A Community College Dropout: Featuring Caesar" by Dave and Mahoney Radio only add fuel to the fire, making it seem like attending a community college is more of a punchline than a legitimate pathway to success. It's as if going to a community college is the educational equivalent of eating the last slice of pizza—sure, it's still pizza, but somehow people act like it's not as good.

But here's the truth: this negative view of community colleges is total nonsense, a ridiculous echo of people who don't know what they're talking about. Community colleges are filled with hardworking students who are determined to make something of themselves—and they do! It's not the consolation prize of higher education; it's the secret weapon. So let's stop with the outdated jokes and give community colleges the respect they deserve. After all, those "lower-tier" students might just be your boss one day.

The objective of this book is to evaluate the American community college system, focusing on its history, current status, and challenges: 1) Trace the evolution of community colleges and analyze current enrollment trends, demographics, and program offerings; 2) Assess the impact on local communities and their role in promoting equity and access; 3) Examine key challenges such as funding constraints, student retention, technological adaptation, and equitable education; 4) Address student-specific challenges, including financial constraints, academic preparation, balancing responsibilities, navigating transfers, limited resources, social integration, retention rates, public perception, and demographic diversity; and 5) Evaluate policies and initiatives, including funding mechanisms and free community college programs, and propose recommendations to enhance effectiveness and sustainability. This paper aims to comprehensively evaluate the American community college system, addressing its evolution, current state, challenges, student issues, and policy recommendations to enhance effectiveness and sustainability.

The American Community College system has been shaped by numerous key pioneers whose contributions have been pivotal in its development. William Rainey Harper, often regarded as the father of the junior college movement, was the first president of the University of Chicago and established the first junior college in Joliet, Illinois, in 1901 (Baker, 2002; Curtis, 1960; Crosby, 1930; Gleazer, 1986; Harper, 1901; Huddleston, 2000; Montag, 1951; Pleasants, 1975; Riggs, 1985; Schultz, 1990). He envisioned junior colleges as institutions that would bridge the gap between high school and university education, providing accessible education to a broader population (Baker, 2002). Myrtle A. Curtis was a key advocate for the development of junior colleges in California, helping to shape the California Master Plan for Higher Education, which established a tiered system of higher education in the state, including community colleges as a crucial component (Crosby, 1930; Gleazer, 1986; Harper, 1901).

"I find that the harder I work, the more luck I seem to have."
~Thomas Jefferson

Leon T. Pleasants played a significant role in expanding community colleges in the Midwest, promoting the idea that community colleges should serve academic and vocational training needs (Pleasants, 1975; Riggs, 1985; Schultz, 1990). John W. Riggs was a leader in the national movement to establish community colleges, serving as the president of the American Association of Junior Colleges (now the American Association of Community Colleges) and working tirelessly to promote federal support and funding for community colleges (Baker, 2002; Harper, 1901; Huddleston, 2000; Montag, 1951). Eells Walter Crosby, a prominent educational theorist, wrote extensively about the role of junior colleges in American education, providing a theoretical foundation for expanding and developing the community college system (Gleazer, 1986; Huddleston, 2000; Riggs, 1985; Schultz, 1990).

Edmund J. Gleazer Jr. served as the president of the American Association of Community Colleges for over two decades, advocating for the role of community colleges in providing accessible education and securing federal support through initiatives like the Higher Education Act of 1965 (Baker, 2002; Curtis, 1960; Gleazer, 1986; Huddleston, 2000; Pleasants, 1975; Riggs, 1985; Schultz, 1990). Raymond E. Schultz was a pioneer in integrating technical and vocational education into the community college curriculum, broadening the scope and appeal of community colleges (Baker, 2002;

Gleazer, 1986; Huddleston, 2000; Riggs, 1985; Schultz, 1990). Dr. Mildred Montag was significant in the development of nursing education within community colleges, advocating for associate degree nursing programs and establishing community colleges as key institutions for training healthcare professionals (Baker, 2002). Dr. George A. Baker III, as a scholar and educator, has contributed extensively to the literature on community college leadership and administration, providing valuable insights into effective practices and policies for community colleges (Baker, 2002; Schultz, 1990).

These pioneers, among others, have laid the foundation for the modern community college system, shaping it into an essential component of American higher education that provides accessible, affordable, and flexible education to millions of students. Their vision has ensured that community colleges serve as gateways for diverse populations, including non-traditional students and those seeking to improve their employment opportunities. By prioritizing inclusivity and community engagement, these institutions have become responsive to local educational and economic needs, offering a wide range of programs from academic transfer pathways to vocational training.

"Genius is 10% inspiration, 90% perspiration." ~*Thomas Edison*

The expansion and growth of American community colleges saw significant acceleration following World War II. This period marked a turning point in higher education, driven by several key factors. The Servicemen's Readjustment Act of 1944, commonly known as the GI Bill, provided educational benefits to returning veterans. This legislation played a pivotal role in increasing college enrollments, as millions of veterans sought to continue their education. Community colleges were well-positioned to meet this demand due to their open admissions policies, lower tuition costs, and local accessibility. They became an essential pathway for veterans transitioning to civilian life and further education (Gilbert & Heller, 2013).

The post-war economic boom created a high demand for skilled labor. Community colleges expanded their vocational and technical programs to train individuals for the burgeoning industrial and service sectors. These institutions provided flexible, short-term training programs that aligned with the needs of local economies, thereby becoming integral to workforce development (Cohen, Brawer, & Kisker, 2014). The societal push towards greater educational access and equity also fueled the growth of community colleges. There was a growing recognition of the need to provide educational opportunities to a broader segment of the population, including non-traditional students, minorities, and women. Community colleges, with their inclusive missions, were at the forefront of this educational democratization (Bailey, Jenkins, & Leinbach, 2005).

The 1960s and 1970s represented a period of remarkable expansion for community colleges, characterized by rapid growth in the number of institutions and enrollments. During this era, federal and state governments increasingly recognized the value of community colleges and provided substantial support for their development. The Higher Education Act of 1965 included provisions for community colleges, offering financial assistance and promoting their role in the broader higher education system. State governments also played a crucial role by establishing new community colleges and expanding existing ones to meet the educational needs of their populations (Beach, 2011).

"Motivation is what gets you started. Habit is what keeps you going."
~Jim Ryun

The social movements of the 1960s, including the civil rights movement and the women's liberation movement, emphasized the importance of equal access to education. Community colleges responded by expanding their programs and services to accommodate a more diverse student body. This period saw an influx of first-generation college students, women returning to education, and minority students seeking higher education opportunities (Cohen, Brawer, & Kisker, 2014). Community colleges began to diversify their curricula to address the changing needs of society. They expanded beyond traditional academic programs to include a wide range of vocational, technical, and adult education programs. This diversification made community colleges more attractive to a broader audience and helped them fulfill their mission of serving the community's educational and workforce needs (Brint & Karabel, 1989).

The physical infrastructure of community colleges expanded significantly during this time. Many new campuses were established, and existing ones were enlarged to accommodate the growing student population. This growth in infrastructure was often supported by state funding and bond measures, reflecting the public's commitment to expanding access to higher education (Gilbert & Heller, 2013).

Community colleges continued to embrace open admissions policies, ensuring that higher education was accessible to all individuals regardless of their academic backgrounds. This commitment to open access distinguished community colleges from other higher education institutions and contributed to their rapid growth and popularity (Bailey, Jenkins, & Leinbach, 2005).

"Success is the sum of small efforts, repeated." ~R. Collier

The post-World War II era and the subsequent decades of the 1960s and 1970s were transformative for American community colleges. These institutions expanded rapidly, driven by societal needs, government support, and a commitment to providing accessible, affordable, and relevant education to a diverse population. As a result, community colleges became a cornerstone of the American higher education system, playing a vital role in promoting social mobility, workforce development, and lifelong learning.

The 21st century has seen significant evolution in community colleges, driven by technological advancements, changing societal needs, and shifts in educational paradigms. One of the most notable developments has been the integration of technology into the classroom. Community colleges have increasingly adopted online learning platforms, hybrid courses, and digital resources to enhance the accessibility and flexibility of education. This shift has been particularly beneficial for non-traditional students, such as working adults and those with family responsibilities, allowing them to balance their studies with other commitments (Smith, 2020).

Community colleges have expanded their role in workforce development. They have formed partnerships with local industries and businesses to create specialized training programs that align with regional economic needs. These programs are designed to equip students with the skills required for high-demand jobs, thereby directly contributing to local economic growth. This focus on workforce development has been crucial in areas experiencing economic transitions, such as shifts from manufacturing to technology-based industries (Jones, 2019).

Recent trends in community colleges reflect a dynamic response to both opportunities and challenges. One significant trend is the emphasis on student success and completion. Community colleges are implementing various strategies to improve graduation rates, such as guided pathways, which provide students with a structured approach to their education, including clear roadmaps for completing degrees or certificates. Enhanced advising, tutoring services, and support programs for first-generation and low-income students are also part of this effort to boost student outcomes (Bailey, Jaggars, & Jenkins, 2015).

"The best way to predict your future is to create it." ~Abraham Lincoln

The demographic composition of community college students is also changing. There is a growing population of older adults returning to education to update their skills or change careers. Additionally, community colleges are seeing an increase in dual enrollment programs, where high school students take college courses to earn credits before graduating. These programs help bridge the gap between secondary and higher education, providing students with a head start on their college education and reducing the overall time and cost required to earn a degree (Karp, 2012).

Financial sustainability remains a critical issue for community colleges. With fluctuating state funding and the rising cost of education, many institutions are exploring alternative funding sources, such as grants, private donations, and partnerships with businesses. Efforts to advocate for increased federal support are also ongoing, particularly in light of the crucial role community colleges play in providing accessible education and training (American Association of Community Colleges, 2021).

Another trend is the growing focus on equity and inclusion. Community colleges are implementing policies and practices aimed at closing achievement gaps among different student groups. Initiatives such as culturally responsive teaching, targeted support services, and efforts to diversify faculty and staff are being adopted to create a more inclusive and supportive educational environment (Santiago, 2018). The modern era of community colleges is characterized by technological integration, a strong emphasis on workforce development, and a commitment to student success and equity. These institutions continue to evolve to meet the changing needs of society and remain vital components of the American higher education system.

Evolution of the American Community College Offering Bachelor's Degrees

American community colleges are increasingly filling the gap left by traditional universities by offering workforce-connected bachelor's degrees. These institutions provide accessible and affordable education closely aligned with local and regional job market needs. By developing programs in high-demand fields such as healthcare, information technology, and business management, community colleges ensure that their graduates possess the practical skills and knowledge required by employers (College Values Online, 2024; U.S. Bureau of Labor Statistics, 2024).

"I've seen with my own students, community colleges offer an affordable route to four-year college degrees and good paying jobs" ~Jill Biden

Community colleges have the flexibility to respond quickly to evolving industry requirements, often partnering with local businesses and organizations to design curricula that address specific workforce needs. This approach not only enhances the employability of graduates but also supports economic development within the community. Additionally, community colleges often offer more flexible scheduling options, including evening, weekend, and online classes, which cater to non-traditional students balancing work and family responsibilities (American Association of Community Colleges, 2021).

While community colleges can respond quickly to evolving industry requirements, this adaptability isn't always reflected in every aspect of their teaching. I've seen firsthand how some faculty members, despite being in an environment that encourages innovation, have become stuck in their ways. Instead of updating their materials and keeping pace with the latest developments, they rely on the same notes, PowerPoint slides, and even transparencies they've been using for decades.

This lack of true professional development leads to some embarrassing moments in the classroom. For instance, I've personally seen faculty members teaching the long-disproved theory that the viceroy butterfly avoids being eaten by mimicking the coloration of two other butterflies that birds dislike. Despite research having debunked this myth years ago—showing that the viceroy is just as unpalatable as its look-alikes—these professors continued to present it as scientific fact. It was like watching someone proudly demonstrate the use of a rotary phone while the rest of the world had moved on to smartphones.

Instead of getting a fresh, up-to-date education, students end up with a history lesson in outdated practices. It's like showing up to a gourmet dinner, only to find the chef serving recipes from a 1970s cookbook. Sure, it's nostalgic, but it's not what today's students need to succeed.

The affordability of community college programs makes higher education accessible to a broader population, reducing financial barriers that might otherwise prevent individuals from pursuing a bachelor's degree. States like Florida and California have been at the forefront of this movement, authorizing community colleges to confer bachelor's degrees in fields with significant workforce demand and a shortage of qualified professionals (Bragg & Durham, 2012).

Community colleges offering bachelor's degrees play a crucial role in enhancing accessibility, affordability, flexibility, and alignment with workforce needs compared to traditional universities. These institutions are often located in underserved or rural areas, making higher education more accessible to local residents who might otherwise face geographic and financial barriers. This accessibility is particularly beneficial for non-traditional students, such as working adults and those with family responsibilities, who may find it challenging to relocate or commute to distant universities. The lower tuition costs at community colleges provide a more affordable pathway to a bachelor's degree, reducing the financial burden on students and their families and potentially leading to lower student debt (U.S. Department of Education, 2020).

Moreover, community colleges frequently design their programs in collaboration with local industries and employers, ensuring that their education aligns with regional workforce needs. By offering bachelor's degrees, community colleges can create targeted programs that address specific skills gaps in the local economy, enhancing employability and meeting job market demands more effectively (American Association of Community Colleges, 2021).

Community colleges are deeply integrated into their local communities, fostering a supportive environment that benefits students academically and professionally. Offering bachelor's degrees allows students to stay within their supportive local networks while pursuing higher education. In comparison, while universities offer a wider range of resources, research opportunities, and programs, they can be more expensive and less accessible to certain populations.

Universities often have more rigorous admissions criteria and larger class sizes, which can be disadvantage for some students who might thrive in a more personalized learning environment provided by community colleges (Bragg & Durham, 2012).

By offering bachelor's degrees, community colleges provide inclusive, affordable, and flexible education options tailored to meet the needs of their local communities and economies, complementing the offerings of traditional universities. This integration of community colleges into the higher education landscape enhances the overall accessibility and responsiveness of the education system to diverse student populations and regional workforce requirements (U.S. Department of Education, 2020).

Increasing Accessibility and Affordability

One of the primary motivations for community colleges to offer bachelor's degrees is to increase access to higher education, particularly for underserved and non-traditional student populations. Community colleges are often more accessible geographically, as they are located within local communities, making it easier for students who have work or family commitments to attend. Additionally, community colleges typically offer more flexible schedules, including night and weekend classes, which cater to working students and those with other responsibilities (Community College Review, 2023).

The cost of obtaining a bachelor's degree at a community college is significantly lower than at traditional four-year universities. This affordability makes higher education attainable for students who might otherwise be deterred by the high cost of tuition at four-year institutions. For instance, states like California have introduced programs where students can earn a bachelor's degree at a community college for a fraction of the cost, reducing the financial burden and potential student debt (Community College Review, 2023).

Addressing Workforce Needs

Community colleges have tailored their bachelor's degree programs to meet specific local and regional workforce needs. Programs are often focused on high-demand fields such as nursing, applied technology, and education. By offering bachelor's degrees in these areas, community colleges help to fill critical gaps in the labor market and provide students with the skills necessary to secure well-paying jobs. For example, the Florida legislature allowed community colleges to offer bachelor's degrees to address the shortage of nurses and teachers, thereby directly contributing to the state's workforce development (New America, 2023). More importantly, faculty and leadership need to be working with industry partners to make successful connections.

The pace at which community colleges are adapting to real-world needs is moving about as fast as a sloth in a marathon, and the programs they offer often miss the mark when it comes to real-world relevance. Take my college, for example. They proudly rolled out a Certificate of Achievement in Cultural Resources Management. Sounds fancy, right? But here's the kicker—in the real world, that certificate is about as useful as a chocolate teapot. To even qualify for the most basic field job, like being a "shovel bum" digging 1 by 1 units on an archaeological site, you need at least a bachelor's degree in anthropology. This certification is nothing more than a desperate attempt by a faculty member to stay relevant, despite being out of touch with what the job market actually requires.

And just when you thought it couldn't get any more ridiculous, they went ahead and created a certificate program in Forensic Anthropology. Now, unless you plan on solving crimes with a magnifying glass and a copy of "CSI for Dummies," this certificate isn't going to get you very far—because to work in this field, you actually need a master's degree. It's like they're selling tickets to a magic show where the only trick is making your career prospects disappear. These programs are essentially selling worthless certifications to students, giving them a diploma in false hope for a job they'll never be qualified to get. It's like the faculty are more interested in teaching a fun subject than in actually preparing students for a real career. If community colleges want to be taken seriously, they need to stop peddling these academic souvenirs and start focusing on programs that will actually help students land jobs in the real world.

Flexible and Localized Education

Another advantage of community college bachelor's degree programs is their flexibility and relevance to local economic needs. These programs are designed to be more accessible and convenient for students who might not be able to relocate or commute to a four-year university. This localized approach helps to keep students within their communities, supporting local economies and addressing specific regional employment needs (The Edvocate, 2018).

However, there's a catch—while the flexibility is great, a bunch of general education courses won't get you a job; they'll just get you a front-row seat to the Debt Show. Community colleges need to shift their focus to workforce-ready programs that actually equip students with skills employers are looking for, or on seamless transfer degrees that truly guarantee a smooth transition to a four-year institution. Otherwise, students are left holding a pile of credits that are about as useful as a screen door on a submarine—great for sinking into debt, but not so much for getting a job. It's a surefire way to put students at a disadvantage both professionally and financially.

Challenges and Considerations

While the expansion of bachelor's degree programs at community colleges has numerous benefits, it also presents challenges. These institutions must navigate the complexities of accreditation and ensure that their programs meet the same standards as those offered by traditional four-year institutions. This often requires significant investment in faculty development, infrastructure, and student support services (New America, 2023).

In summary, community colleges are now offering bachelor's degrees to make higher education more accessible and affordable, meet local workforce needs, and provide flexible educational options for non-traditional students. This trend is transforming higher education by creating viable pathways for students to achieve their academic and career goals without the financial and logistical barriers often associated with traditional four-year institutions.

But never have I ever heard a senior manager respond to a division head with, "What if we succeed?" uttered with sheer terror in their eyes—like they'd just seen a ghost holding a performance review. This amusing yet revealing reaction really highlights the innovative and sometimes totally unexpected changes that community colleges are bringing to the higher education landscape. If we fail, the students fail—what a groundbreaking revelation—making our success not just desirable, but absolutely essential for the future of our students and communities. Because, obviously, doing our jobs well is of utmost importance.

Chapter 2

Blueprints of Community College Governance

T he organizational structure of a community college is designed to ensure effective administration, academic management, and support services. Typically, it includes several key components: the Board of Trustees, responsible for the overall strategic direction and policy-making of the college; the President, who oversees daily operations, implements board policies, and provides leadership; Vice Presidents or Provosts, who manage specific areas such as academic affairs, student services, finance, and administration; Deans, responsible for specific academic divisions or departments like humanities, sciences, or vocational programs; Faculty, who deliver the educational programs and engage in curriculum development; and Support Staff, providing essential services such as admissions, advising, financial aid, and facilities management (Cohen, Brawer, & Kisker, 2014).

Community colleges in the United States operate under various governance models, each reflecting the specific needs and contexts of their states and communities. The primary models include the State Governance Model, where the state government exerts significant control through a state board of education or higher education commission, setting policies, allocating funding, and overseeing college operations to ensure alignment with state educational goals; and the Local Governance Model, which involves a locally elected or appointed board of trustees with substantial autonomy over the college's operations, finances, and policies, allowing for greater responsiveness to local community needs and priorities (American Association of Community Colleges, 2021).

"Community colleges are the great American invention in terms of education"
~Eduardo J. Padron

The balance between state and local governance can vary widely. Under state governance, the state government provides the majority of funding and regulatory oversight, ensuring consistency across institutions within the state and facilitating statewide initiatives and standardization. However, this model may also limit the flexibility of individual colleges to respond to local needs. In contrast, locally governed systems grant community colleges greater independence to tailor their programs and services to the specific needs of their communities. Local boards of trustees make decisions on budgeting, curriculum, and strategic planning, offering flexibility and local control but potentially resulting in variability in quality and resources among colleges within the same state (Bailey, Jaggars, & Jenkins, 2015).

The Board of Trustees plays a crucial role in the governance and strategic direction of community colleges. Their responsibilities include policymaking, financial oversight, hiring and evaluation, strategic planning, and advocacy. Effective boards establish policies that guide the college's operations, approve budgets to ensure fiscal health, appoint and evaluate key administrators, set long-term goals, and represent the college in the broader community (Smith, 2020).

Administrative Structure

The administrative structure of a community college is designed to facilitate effective governance, management, and delivery of educational services. At the top of this hierarchy is the Board of Trustees, the governing body responsible for setting policies, approving budgets, hiring the president, and overseeing the overall strategic direction of the college. The president, acting as the chief executive officer, implements board policies, oversees daily operations, provides leadership, and represents the college in the community (Cohen, Brawer, & Kisker, 2014).

Supporting the president are several vice presidents or provosts, each managing specific areas such as academic affairs, student services, finance and administration, and institutional advancement. The vice president for academic affairs manages academic programs, curriculum development, faculty hiring, and accreditation processes, while the vice president for student services oversees admissions, counseling, student activities, and support services aimed at student success. The vice president for finance and administration handles budgeting, financial planning, facilities management, and administrative support, and the vice president for institutional advancement focuses on fundraising, public relations, and community outreach (Bailey, Jaggars, & Jenkins, 2015).

Deans oversee specific academic divisions or departments, such as humanities, sciences, or vocational programs, ensuring quality education and compliance with academic standards. Directors and managers head various administrative departments, such as human resources, IT, library services, and continuing education, providing essential support to the college's operations. Faculty members deliver educational programs, engage in curriculum development, and contribute to the academic mission through teaching, research, and service. Support staff provide essential services including admissions, advising, financial aid, and facilities management, ensuring the smooth functioning of the college (Smith, 2020).

"The future belongs to those who believe in the beauty of their dreams."
~Eleanor Roosevelt

Community colleges may adopt different organizational models based on their size, mission, and governance structure. In a centralized model, decision-making authority is concentrated at the top levels of administration, ensuring consistency in policies and procedures, streamlined decision-making, and clear accountability. However, this model may lack flexibility and responsiveness to specific departmental or local needs. In contrast, a decentralized model distributes decision-making authority across various levels of the institution, giving more autonomy to deans, directors, and department heads. This model offers greater flexibility and responsiveness but can lead to inconsistency in policies and procedures. A matrix model combines elements of both centralized and decentralized structures, balancing consistency with flexibility and encouraging collaboration across departments, although it can create complexity in management and potential conflicts in authority (American Association of Community Colleges, 2021).

Funding and Financial Management

Community colleges face several funding and financial management issues that impact their ability to deliver quality education and services. These issues are often tied to the sources of funding, budgeting practices, and the financial challenges unique to these institutions. Community colleges receive funding from various sources, each contributing to their overall financial health. State governments provide a significant portion of community college funding, which is critical for maintaining operations and keeping tuition affordable. However, state funding can fluctuate based on economic conditions and political priorities, leading to financial instability (Cohen, Brawer, & Kisker, 2014).

The federal government offers financial support through grants, such as the Pell Grant program, which assists low-income students. Federal funds also come from various initiatives aimed at workforce development and special projects. While helpful, federal funding is often targeted and may not cover general operational expenses (American Association of Community Colleges, 2021). Tuition and fees paid by students are a vital source of revenue for community colleges. These institutions strive to keep tuition low to remain accessible, which can limit the amount of revenue generated. Financial aid and scholarships help mitigate costs for students but also affect the net revenue collected from tuition (Bailey, Jaggars, & Jenkins, 2015).

Budgeting and financial management in community colleges involve addressing several challenges. Dependence on state and local funding, which can be unpredictable and subject to cuts, poses a significant challenge. Colleges must often adjust their budgets with little notice, impacting program offerings and staffing levels (Cohen, Brawer, & Kisker, 2014). Operating costs, including salaries, benefits, maintenance, and technology, continue to rise. Balancing these costs while maintaining affordability for students requires careful financial planning and often difficult trade-offs (Smith, 2020). Managing financial aid effectively is crucial for community colleges. Ensuring that students receive timely and adequate support while maintaining compliance with federal regulations adds to the administrative burden (American Association of Community Colleges, 2021).

State	Community Colleges per Credit Hour	Universities per Credit Hour
California	$46	$370
Texas	$85	$300
Florida	$104	$200
New York	$195	$300
Illinois	$150	$400
Pennsylvania	$190	$450
Ohio	$135	$350
Georgia	$95	$400
N. Carolina	$76	$300
Michigan	$110	$420
Nevada	$105	$320

Instate cost, N. Center for Education Statistics. (2023); College Board. (2023)

Community Colleges Shortfalls Compared to Universities

Community colleges often face financial shortfalls compared to four-year universities, which can significantly affect their ability to provide comparable services and facilities. Community colleges typically receive less funding per student than universities, limiting their ability to invest in advanced facilities, technology, and extensive support services (Bailey, Jaggars, & Jenkins, 2015). This disparity in funding means that community colleges may struggle to maintain modern campuses, invest in state-of-the-art laboratories, or provide the latest technology for their students and faculty. Unlike universities, community colleges receive little to no funding for research activities. This limitation impacts their ability to attract faculty and students interested in research and innovation, as there are fewer opportunities for research grants, academic publications, and cutting-edge projects (Cohen, Brawer, & Kisker, 2014).

The financial constraints of community colleges often result in less developed infrastructure and fewer resources for students and faculty. This includes fewer extracurricular activities, less comprehensive libraries, and older facilities. The limited budget may force community colleges to cut back on student services such as career counseling, mental health support, and extracurricular programs that enhance the overall college experience (Smith, 2020). Additionally, community colleges may not be able to offer as many specialized programs or advanced courses, limiting the educational opportunities available to students.

"You are braver than you believe, stronger than you seem and smarter than you think." ~A.A. Milne

Despite these challenges, community colleges continue to play a crucial role in higher education by providing accessible, affordable education and training to a diverse student population. They serve as an essential gateway for many students, including non-traditional students, first-generation college students, and those from low-income backgrounds, offering a pathway to higher education and improved career prospects. Addressing funding and financial management issues is essential to enhance their ability to serve students and communities effectively. Increased financial support from state and federal governments, along with innovative funding strategies, can help bridge the gap and enable community colleges to continue fulfilling their vital educational mission.

Ultimately, addressing the complexities of community college cost requires a multifaceted approach. Rising tuition costs, driven by reductions in state funding, present significant barriers for students, particularly those from working-class backgrounds. The financial aid system, while beneficial, often falls short due to eligibility requirements and a lack of awareness among students. Hidden costs such as fees, textbooks, and transportation further strain student finances. Additionally, the inconsistency in transfer credit policies leads to extended and more costly education pathways. Economic challenges and demographic factors have also significantly impacted enrollment and completion rates, as seen during the Great Recession and the COVID-19 pandemic. To improve access and success, comprehensive policy changes, increased funding, and better support systems are essential to ensure community colleges can continue to serve as a vital educational resource. Again, if we fail, our students fail, making our success not just desirable but crucial for the future of our students and communities.

Failures of State-Elected Boards in Controlling Community Colleges

The failures of a state-elected board in controlling community colleges often stem from political influence, lack of expertise, and misaligned priorities. Political influence can lead to frequent policy changes and instability, as board members may prioritize political agendas over educational needs. For instance, in Connecticut, political motivations have led to the creation of redundant administrative offices, diverting funds away from essential student services and causing significant budget cuts for individual colleges (Connecticut Mirror, 2023). Additionally, the selection process for board members often emphasizes political connections over relevant experience, leading to poor decision-making and inadequate oversight (Education NC, 2023; Inside Higher Ed, 2023).

I've seen this firsthand at the institution I'm at, especially when it comes to picking our president. It's like watching a reality TV show where the winner is chosen based on political connections and whatever happens to be the "flavor of the year," rather than on who's actually best for the job. Instead of getting someone who understands higher education, we end up with a leader who's more focused on politics or following the latest trend than on what's best for the college.

But it doesn't stop there—once a poor leader is in place, they tend to hire even more poor leaders, creating a sort of "mediocrity bubble" where no one's allowed to be too good, just in case they accidentally outshine the boss. It's like assembling a team of B-list actors for a blockbuster movie—you're not going to win any Oscars, but at least no one's going to steal the spotlight! This merry band of underwhelming leaders spends more time making sure they don't look bad than actually moving the college forward. Meanwhile, the rest of us are left to wonder how we ended up in this sitcom where the only plot twist is the next poor decision.

In summary, community colleges are now offering bachelor's degrees to make higher education more accessible and affordable, meet local workforce needs, and provide flexible educational options for non-traditional students. This trend is transforming higher education by creating viable pathways for students to achieve their academic and career goals without the financial and logistical barriers often associated with traditional four-year institutions.

But never have I ever heard a senior manager respond to a division head with, "What if we succeed?" uttered with sheer terror in their eyes—like they'd just seen a ghost holding a performance review. This amusing yet revealing reaction underscores the innovative and sometimes unexpected changes that community colleges are bringing to the higher education landscape.

However, funding and resource allocation remain problematic. Politically driven decisions often result in the misallocation of resources, with funds directed toward politically favorable projects rather than critical educational needs. This inconsistency in funding priorities can cause financial instability for community colleges. Furthermore, bureaucratic inefficiencies arise as political processes slow down decision-making and the implementation of necessary changes. For instance, in North Carolina, political control over board appointments has led to increased administrative complexity and slowed policy implementation (Education NC, 2023; Inside Higher Ed, 2023). These inefficiencies, coupled with a lack of accountability, allow poor performance to persist without significant consequences, ultimately affecting faculty job security, student outcomes, and the adoption of innovative educational practices.

If we fail, our students fail—shocking, right? This makes our success not just a nice-to-have but absolutely crucial for the future of our students and communities. Who knew? This clearly underscores the importance of effective resource management and accountability, because apparently, those things matter. Ensuring the continued success and growth of community colleges means overcoming challenges, fostering innovation, and maintaining a steadfast commitment to educational excellence. It's almost like doing our jobs well is important or something.

While the official story paints the community college organizational structure as a well-oiled machine, the reality is more like a Rube Goldberg contraption, where you hope the ball lands in the right cup, but it's anybody's guess. Sure, there's the Board of Trustees setting strategic direction and the President keeping the ship sailing, but by the time the message filters down through Vice Presidents, Deans, and faculty, it's often completely garbled—like ordering a pizza and ending up with a fruit salad. Governance models don't help much either; whether the state or a local board is running the show, it's like a tug-of-war where no one's sure which side they're on. The state wants everyone marching in sync, while local governance prefers freestyle swimming, leading to some colleges thriving while others are stuck with chalkboards. Faculty are trying to deliver education while buried under outdated course materials, and support staff are the unsung heroes, keeping things running on a shoestring budget. In the end, while the idealized version of community college governance sounds impressive, the reality is a mix of good intentions, bureaucratic hurdles, and a whole lot of improvisation—but if you can navigate that, you're probably ready for anything!

Chapter 3

Financial Aid abuse by Higher Education

The cost of college in the United States has soared over the past few decades, becoming a significant financial burden for many families. As tuition fees and associated expenses continue to rise, students and their families increasingly rely on financial aid to make higher education accessible. Financial aid, encompassing grants, scholarships, work-study programs, and loans, plays a crucial role in bridging the gap between the rising cost of college and what students can afford to pay. Despite the availability of these resources, navigating the complex landscape of financial aid can be daunting. This financial aid system, while essential, is saddling all college students, especially those in community colleges, with debt they may never be able to pay off. This reality underscores the need for better information and guidance to ensure that all students have the opportunity to pursue their educational goals without incurring insurmountable debt. This chapter goes over the types of aid available to student, the cost associated, and the final impact to community college students.

The Rising Cost of College Education Over the Past 40 Years

Over the past four decades, the cost of college education in the United States has increased at an alarming rate, outpacing both inflation and wage growth. In the early 1980s, the average annual tuition for a four-year public university was around $1,000, while private institutions charged approximately $5,000. By the 2020s, these figures had skyrocketed to nearly $10,000 for public universities and over $35,000 for private colleges, excluding room, board, and other fees. This exponential rise can be attributed to various factors, including decreased state funding for public universities, increased demand for higher education, and rising administrative and operational costs.

Decreased State Funding

One of the primary drivers of increased tuition costs is the significant reduction in state funding for public universities. In the 1980s, state governments covered a substantial portion of the costs of public higher education. However, over the years, budget cuts and shifting priorities have led to a decline in state contributions. According to the Center on Budget and Policy Priorities, state funding for public colleges and universities remains well below historical levels, with average state funding per student falling by more than 13% from 2008 to 2018 (Center on Budget and Policy Priorities, 2019). This decline forces institutions to raise tuition and fees to make up for the shortfall.

Increased Demand for Higher Education

The demand for higher education has also surged over the past 40 years, driven by a growing recognition of the importance of a college degree for career success and economic mobility. As more students seek college degrees, institutions have expanded their campuses, programs, and services to accommodate the influx. This expansion, while necessary, has contributed to rising operational costs. The National Center for Education Statistics reports that undergraduate enrollment increased by 28% from 2000 to 2018, putting additional pressure on colleges and universities to maintain and upgrade their facilities and resources (National Center for Education Statistics, 2020).

Rising Administrative and Operational Costs

Administrative and operational costs have also played a significant role in driving up tuition fees. Colleges and universities have seen substantial increases in expenditures related to salaries, benefits, technology, and campus infrastructure. The Delta Cost Project found that administrative spending per student grew by 13% at public institutions and by 22% at private institutions between 1990 and 2014 (Delta Cost Project, 2016). Additionally, the costs associated with student services, such as counseling, health services, and extracurricular activities, have risen as institutions strive to provide a comprehensive college experience.

The Financial Impact on Students and Families

As a result of these factors, students and their families are facing unprecedented financial challenges. The increasing reliance on student loans has led to a burgeoning student debt crisis, with the Federal Reserve reporting that Americans owe over $1.7 trillion in student loan debt as of 2021 (Federal Reserve, 2021). This debt burden can have long-term implications, affecting graduates' ability to buy homes, start families, and save for retirement. The escalating costs have sparked widespread debate and concern about the affordability and accessibility of higher education, prompting calls for policy reforms and innovative solutions to address this critical issue.

The rising cost of college education over the past 40 years is a complex issue with multiple contributing factors. Decreased state funding, increased demand for higher education, and rising administrative and operational costs have all played significant roles in driving up tuition fees. As students and their families continue to navigate these financial challenges, it is crucial for policymakers, educators, and stakeholders to work together to find sustainable solutions that ensure access to affordable, high-quality education for all.

Types of Financial Aid Available to College Students

Navigating the financial landscape of higher education can be complex, but understanding the various types of financial aid available can make the process more manageable. Financial aid for college students generally falls into four main categories: grants, scholarships, work-study programs, and loans. Each type has its own eligibility requirements, benefits, and considerations.

Grants

Grants are a form of financial aid that do not need to be repaid, making them highly desirable. They are typically awarded based on financial need, as determined by the Free Application for Federal Student Aid (FAFSA). The most well-known grant is the federal Pell Grant, which is available to undergraduate students who demonstrate exceptional financial need (Federal Student Aid, n.d.-a). Other federal grants include the Federal Supplemental Educational Opportunity Grant (FSEOG), which is for students with significant financial need, and TEACH Grants, which support students who plan to become teachers in high-need fields (Federal Student Aid, n.d.-b). Many states and institutions also offer their own grants to assist students.

Scholarships

Scholarships, like grants, do not require repayment and are awarded based on various criteria, including academic achievement, athletic ability, artistic talent, leadership, and community service. Scholarships can come from a wide range of sources, including colleges and universities, private organizations, non-profits, and corporations (College Board, n.d.). There are also scholarships specifically aimed at particular demographics, such as scholarships for minority students, women, or veterans. Applying for scholarships often involves submitting essays, recommendation letters, and proof of eligibility.

Work-Study Programs

Work-study programs provide students with part-time employment opportunities, often on campus, to help cover educational expenses. These programs are typically need-based and are part of the federal financial aid package (Federal Student Aid, n.d.-c). Students earn money through their work, which can be applied to tuition, books, and other costs. Work-study jobs are often flexible, allowing students to balance their work hours with their academic schedules. These positions can also provide valuable work experience and professional skills.

Loans

Loans are a common form of financial aid that must be repaid with interest. They are available from federal and private sources. Federal student loans, such as Direct Subsidized Loans and Direct Unsubsidized Loans, are typically preferred because they offer lower interest rates and more flexible repayment options compared to private loans. Subsidized loans are need-based, with the government covering the interest while the student is in school, whereas unsubsidized loans are not need-based and accrue interest during all periods (Federal Student Aid, n.d.-d). Another federal option is the Direct PLUS Loan, which is available to graduate students and parents of dependent undergraduates. Private student loans, offered by banks and other financial institutions, usually have higher interest rates and less flexible repayment terms (Consumer Financial Protection Bureau, n.d.).

Understanding the different types of financial aid available is crucial for students and families planning for college expenses. Grants and scholarships offer valuable funding that does not need to be repaid, while work-study programs provide the opportunity to earn money and gain experience. Loans, although they must be repaid with interest, can help bridge the gap between available funds and the cost of education. By exploring all available options and carefully considering the terms and conditions of each type of aid, students can make informed decisions that support their educational goals.

Navigating the Financial Aid Application Process

Navigating the financial aid application process can be a complex and overwhelming task for many students and their families. The first and most crucial step is completing the Free Application for Federal Student Aid (FAFSA), which collects information about the student's and family's financial situation to determine eligibility for various types of aid. Some colleges also require the CSS Profile for a more detailed assessment. Students need to gather key documents such as Social Security numbers, tax returns, and bank statements to complete these applications accurately. Each school and state has its own deadlines, making it vital to check with each institution's financial aid office to ensure timely submission. After submitting the FAFSA, students receive a Student Aid Report (SAR) summarizing their information and Expected Family Contribution (EFC).

Reviewing and correcting the SAR promptly is essential. Once accepted to colleges, students receive financial aid award letters, which they must compare to understand the total cost of attendance. Accepting and finalizing aid involves signing promissory notes for loans and completing any additional requirements specified by the school's financial aid office. Given the intricacies of this process, it is crucial for colleges to take responsibility in guiding students and their families through these steps, providing clear information, resources, and support to ensure they can secure the necessary funding for their education without incurring insurmountable debt.

Balancing Education and Debt: Strategies for Financial Sustainability

Balancing the pursuit of higher education with managing debt is a significant challenge for many students. Developing strategies for financial sustainability is essential. Creating a detailed budget helps track income and expenses, prioritizing essentials such as tuition, books, housing, and food. Actively seeking scholarships and grants, which do not require repayment, can significantly reduce costs. Participating in work-study programs or finding part-time employment provides financial relief and valuable work experience. Choosing affordable education options, like community colleges or in-state public institutions, can minimize borrowing needs. When taking out loans, it is crucial to borrow only what is necessary and understand the terms and conditions. Exploring loan forgiveness programs and income-driven repayment plans can make loan repayment more manageable. Building financial literacy empowers students to make informed decisions about money. Colleges and universities play a critical role by providing financial education and resources to help students navigate the complexities of financing their education.

Financial Impact on Community College Students Who Take Out Loans and Face Academic Challenges

Community college students who take out loans and then face challenges such as not finishing their degree, transferring to a university, or not succeeding after transfer can experience significant financial repercussions. Some of the impacts to community college students who are not success are as follows:

- **Accumulation of Debt Without a Degree:** Students who take out loans but do not complete their degree end up with debt but no credential to show for it. This can severely limit their earning potential, making it harder to repay the loans. According to a report by the Community College Research Center, students who do not complete their degree are more likely to default on their loans compared to those who graduate (Community College Research Center, 2017). This can lead to damaged credit scores, making it difficult to secure future loans, housing, or even employment.

- **Increased Financial Burden Due to Transfer Issues:** Transferring from a community college to a university often involves additional costs and logistical challenges. Credits may not fully transfer, requiring students to retake courses, which increases both time and financial investment. This can result in taking out more loans to cover the extended period of study (American Council on Education, 2018). Furthermore, the transition can be stressful, and any academic difficulties during this period can compound financial strain.

- **Higher Costs and Loans at Universities:** After transferring, students typically face higher tuition fees and living costs at universities compared to community colleges. If they are not academically successful, they may end up taking longer to complete their degree, further increasing their loan amounts. This extended time in school, coupled with higher expenses, exacerbates their debt situation. Additionally, students who struggle academically might lose eligibility for scholarships or grants, leading them to rely even more heavily on loans (National Student Clearinghouse Research Center, 2020).

- **Limited Employment Opportunities:** Without a completed degree or with a poor academic record, students might struggle to find well-paying jobs that can support loan repayment. Many employers look for candidates with completed degrees or a strong academic track record, and students who fall short may find themselves underemployed or in lower-paying jobs. This situation makes it difficult to manage and repay student loans, often leading to financial distress (Georgetown University Center on Education and the Workforce, 2019).

- **Psychological and Emotional Stress:** The financial strain of accumulating debt without the intended educational outcomes can also lead to significant psychological and emotional stress. This stress can affect overall well-being and hinder the ability to focus on academic or career advancement, creating a vicious cycle of financial and personal difficulties (American Psychological Association, 2019).

The student loan crisis in the United States has evolved into a national catastrophe, impacting millions of borrowers and posing significant challenges to the country's economic stability. Over the past few decades, the cost of higher education has soared, far outpacing inflation and wage growth. According to the College Board, the average tuition and fees at public four-year institutions have increased by more than 200% since the 1980s (College Board, 2020; Mitchell, 2021). This dramatic rise has made it increasingly difficult for families to afford college without taking on substantial debt. Financial aid policies have not kept pace with the escalating costs. Pell Grants, which once covered nearly 80% of the cost of attending a public four-year institution, now cover less than 30% (National Center for Education Statistics, 2020; Mitchell, 2021). This gap has forced students to rely heavily on loans to finance their education. As a result, Americans owe over $1.7 trillion in student loans, affecting more than 44 million borrowers (Federal Reserve, 2021). The burden of this debt has significant implications for individual borrowers and the broader economy, as it reduces consumer spending and hampers economic growth.

Community college students are particularly entrapped in this game of legal debtors. These students often come from lower-income backgrounds and see community colleges as a more affordable entry point into higher education. However, many face additional challenges such as part-time enrollment, working while studying, and family responsibilities, which can prolong their education journey and increase the likelihood of taking out loans. Moreover, transferring to a four-year university often results in additional costs and logistical challenges, with credits not always fully transferring, necessitating retaking courses and extending the time and money spent on education (American Council on Education, 2018; Mitchell, 2021). This situation exacerbates the financial burden, especially for those who do not complete their degrees or who struggle academically after transfer. The complexity and inadequacies of the financial aid system further entrap these students, disproportionately affecting vulnerable populations, including low-income, first-generation, and minority students. Addressing this crisis requires comprehensive reforms to make higher education more affordable and accessible, including increasing funding for grants, controlling tuition costs, and simplifying loan repayment and forgiveness processes.

Let's face it: when it comes to financial aid, higher education institutions are like the overzealous friend who insists on reminding you how great they are at their job, even when it's just about collecting cash. We proudly brag about the impressive amount of financial aid we're wrangling from students, as if we're in a competitive sport with other colleges. Meanwhile, talking about student success is a distant afterthought, like dessert at a buffet that's been left out a little too long. At my institution, we have an uncanny ability to turn financial aid into a dazzling display of our money-grabbing prowess, while the whole success narrative is left sitting quietly in the corner, waiting for its turn in the spotlight. It's like hosting a party where the only thing people remember is how much they paid to get in, not the actual fun they had.

Chapter 4

Guiding Success: Leadership in Community Colleges

L eadership in community colleges is like being the ringmaster in a circus—minus the top hat and lions. These leaders are crucial for shaping the institution's vision, mission, and strategic direction, basically deciding whether the college is going to soar like an eagle or flop like a pancake. Effective leaders set the tone and culture of the college, establishing goals and guiding the institution toward achieving them, all while juggling flaming torches and riding a unicycle. They create an environment that fosters academic excellence, student success, and community engagement, kind of like turning water into wine but with less divine intervention. This involves developing policies and practices that promote high-quality teaching and learning, ensuring students get the support and resources they need to succeed academically and personally (Cohen, Brawer, & Kisker, 2014). Because nothing says "we care" like a policy that finally lets you find the right classroom without needing a map and a Sherpa.

While the idea of developing policies to promote high-quality teaching and learning sounds like a dream come true, in reality, it often turns into a never-ending episode of "Policy and Procedure Limbo." Instead of improving anything, these policies can end up as bureaucratic spaghetti, tangling up faculty in so much red tape that they spend more time filling out forms and attending meetings than actually teaching. Meanwhile, students are left trying to find the resources they need, like they're on a scavenger hunt with no map and a broken compass. What was supposed to make education better somehow turns into a game of "How Low Can You Go?"—with faculty and students trying to navigate under a bar that keeps getting lower. So, while these policies might look great in a glossy brochure, in reality, they often end up being more about keeping up appearances than actually helping anyone succeed.

However, community colleges are often lacking in solid leadership due to career turfing, personal goals, nepotism, and a "do whatever it takes to get what you want" mentality. It's as if some leaders are more interested in climbing the career ladder than actually helping students climb their own educational ladders. Nepotism and personal agendas can turn decision-making into a game of "who you know" rather than "what's best for students." With a focus on personal gain over student success, it's no wonder some colleges struggle to maintain a coherent vision and mission. It's hard to steer the ship when everyone's too busy fighting over who gets to be captain, rather than making sure the students don't end up overboard.

"Leadership and learning: "Leadership and learning are indispensable to each other" ~John F. Kennedy.

Leaders in community colleges must navigate the complexities of managing diverse student populations, faculty, and staff. This includes understanding and addressing the unique needs of non-traditional students, such as adult learners, first-generation college students, and those from various socio-economic backgrounds. It also involves fostering an inclusive and supportive campus culture where all members feel valued and are encouraged to contribute to the college's mission (Cohen, Brawer, & Kisker, 2014).

Additionally, community college leaders are tasked with ensuring the institution meets its educational and financial goals. This requires strategic planning, resource management, and the ability to adapt to changing circumstances. Leaders must be adept at securing funding from various sources, including state and federal governments, grants, and private donations, to maintain financial stability and support institutional growth. They must also be capable of making difficult decisions regarding budgeting and resource allocation to maximize the college's impact on student success and community development (Bailey, Jaggars, & Jenkins, 2015).

Effective leadership is essential in educational institutions to drive positive outcomes and continuous improvement. Leaders in community colleges play a pivotal role in influencing the quality of education, operational efficiency, and overall institutional reputation. By setting clear goals and expectations, they ensure that educational standards are met and often exceeded, fostering an environment where both students and faculty can thrive (Bailey, Jaggars, & Jenkins, 2015).

Leaders inspire and motivate faculty and staff by creating a shared vision and fostering a sense of purpose. This motivation is crucial for maintaining high levels of engagement and productivity. When faculty and staff are inspired, they are more likely to innovate in their teaching methods, seek professional development opportunities, and contribute positively to the college community. Effective leaders recognize and reward these efforts, which helps build a culture of excellence and continuous improvement (Bailey, Jaggars, & Jenkins, 2015).

Promoting innovation is another critical aspect of leadership in community colleges. Leaders encourage experimentation with new teaching techniques, the integration of technology in the classroom, and the development of programs that meet the evolving needs of students and the community. This innovative mindset ensures that the institution remains relevant and capable of providing high-quality education that prepares students for the future. Leaders who embrace change and foster a culture of innovation are better positioned to adapt to the fast-paced developments in education and technology (Smith, 2020).

Cultivating a culture of collaboration and accountability is also essential for effective leadership. Leaders in community colleges work to create an environment where faculty and staff feel valued and empowered to contribute their ideas and expertise. This collaborative approach leads to more effective problem-solving and decision-making, as diverse perspectives are considered. Additionally, by establishing clear accountability mechanisms, leaders ensure that everyone understands their roles and responsibilities, which helps maintain high standards and achieve institutional goals (Bailey, Jaggars, & Jenkins, 2015).

Strong leadership is vital for adapting to changing educational needs, implementing new technologies, and responding to economic and demographic shifts. The landscape of higher education is continually evolving, with new challenges and opportunities arising regularly. Effective leaders are proactive in identifying trends and anticipating the needs of their students and communities. They invest in professional development for themselves and their staff to stay abreast of the latest educational research and practices (Smith, 2020).

Moreover, leaders must navigate the complexities of economic and demographic shifts that impact enrollment, funding, and resource allocation. For instance, during economic downturns, community colleges often see an increase in enrollment as individuals seek to improve their skills and employability. Leaders must be prepared to accommodate this surge in demand while maintaining the quality of education and services provided. Similarly, demographic changes, such as shifts in population age or diversity, require leaders to adapt their strategies to ensure that all student groups are adequately supported (Cohen, Brawer, & Kisker, 2014).

Effective leadership in community colleges involves employing various styles and strategies to address the unique challenges and opportunities these institutions face. The diversity of the student population, the need for flexible educational pathways, and the requirement to maintain close ties with the community necessitate a dynamic and adaptable leadership approach. Here are some key leadership styles and strategies that are particularly effective in the community college context according to researchers (e.g. Kahneman & Tversky, 1979; Mintzberg, 1994; Porter, 1980; Rumelt, 2011):

- **Transformational Leadership**: Involves inspiring and motivating faculty, staff, and students to achieve their full potential and work towards common goals. Transformational leaders create a vision for the future and foster an environment of innovation and change. They encourage professional development, recognize and reward accomplishments, and build a strong sense of community within the college (Bailey, Jaggars, & Jenkins, 2015).

- **Collaborative Leadership**: Emphasizes the importance of teamwork and collective decision-making. Effective leaders in community colleges often adopt a collaborative approach, encouraging input and participation from various stakeholders, including faculty, staff, students, and community members (Cohen, Brawer, & Kisker, 2014).

- **Servant Leadership**: Focuses on prioritizing the needs of others and serving the institution's community. Servant leaders prioritize the well-being and development of their faculty, staff, and students. This approach fosters a supportive and nurturing environment conducive to personal and professional growth (Smith, 2020).

- **Strategic Planning**: Involves developing and implementing a clear, strategic plan that aligns with the institution's mission and goals. This includes setting long-term objectives, identifying key priorities, and allocating resources effectively. Strategic planning helps ensure that the college can adapt to changing educational needs, economic conditions, and technological advancements (American Association of Community Colleges, 2021).

- **Stakeholder Engagement**: Actively engaging with internal and external stakeholders is essential for effective leadership in community colleges. Leaders must build partnerships with local businesses, government agencies, non-profit organizations, and other educational institutions to create opportunities for students and enhance the college's impact on the community (Cohen, Brawer, & Kisker, 2014).

- **Professional Development**: Investing in the continuous professional development of faculty and staff is a key leadership strategy. Community college leaders must ensure that their teams have access to training, workshops, and other development opportunities that enhance their skills and effectiveness (Smith, 2020).

Leadership Challenges at the Community Colleges

Community college leaders tend to earn online Ed.D. (Doctor of Education) degrees rather than the more "practical" Ed.D. or the traditional Ph.D. (Doctor of Philosophy) degrees. Because, clearly, clicking through PowerPoint slides in your pajamas at home is the pinnacle of educational achievement. Online degrees are frequently criticized for their perceived lack of quality and substance—probably because limited interaction between students and instructors, inadequate hands-on learning experiences, and a potentially less rigorous academic environment just scream "top-notch education" (Levin, 2001; Osguthorpe & Wong, 1993; Perry, 2016). These programs often struggle to provide the same depth of engagement, real-world application, and academic rigor found in traditional, on-campus programs. But hey, who needs all that pesky real-world experience anyway?

On-ground and practical degrees are considered superior because they offer direct interaction with instructors, hands-on learning experiences, and a more rigorous academic environment. These programs provide opportunities for real-time feedback, collaborative learning, and practical application of knowledge, which are essential for deep understanding and skill development.

While I wouldn't say that all online degrees are of poor quality, there's a specific issue with these EdDs in Community College Leadership and Higher Education Administration. They're often marketed as a way to learn how to be a leader, but here's the thing—leaders aren't made, they're born. If someone already has the potential to lead but just needs a little guidance, sure, you can develop that. But trying to teach leadership to someone who doesn't naturally have it? That's like trying to teach a cat to fetch—it's just not going to happen. These degrees promise to mold people into leaders, but the reality is, no amount of coursework can instill the intrinsic qualities of a true leader. While these programs might help polish existing leadership skills, they can't create something out of nothing.

I see so many people at community colleges running down this path, chasing after these leadership degrees in hopes of becoming a VP or President. It's like there's a mad dash to collect these EdDs, thinking they're the golden ticket to the top. But here's the thing—at universities, you almost never see this kind of frenzy for leadership degrees. Why? Because universities know that real leadership isn't something you can just slap a degree on. They need leaders with deep knowledge of their field, people who have proven themselves through years of experience and expertise. That's why they look for leaders within their existing ranks or pluck the best and brightest from other institutions. They're not interested in someone with a shiny new degree in leadership hot off the online university copier; they want someone who's already demonstrated they can lead, someone with the credentials, experience, and respect to take on the role. At universities, it's less about titles and more about substance—something the community college crowd chasing these online leadership degrees might want to consider.

Community college leaders often earn Ed.D. degrees designed to prepare them with a practical focus on administration, policy, and curriculum—basically, all the nuts and bolts of running a college. But let's be real: no degree, no matter how fancy, can turn a non-leader into a leader. You can teach someone how to fill out all the right forms and navigate the red tape, but that doesn't make them the next great visionary. Leadership is something that's discovered and nurtured, not something you pick up in a classroom like a new skill at a weekend workshop.

True leaders have an innate ability to inspire, guide, and make tough decisions—qualities that can't be conjured up through a few semesters of coursework. Sure, an EdD might polish the rough edges of someone who already has leadership potential, but it's not a magic wand. If those leadership traits aren't there to begin with, no degree is going to suddenly make someone the next great college president. Leadership is about more than just knowing the rules; it's about having the character, vision, and ability to rally the troops—traits that can't be printed on a diploma.

During my time in the reserves of the U.S. military, I saw firsthand the diverse range of leadership—and lack thereof—within the officer corps. There were a few solid leaders who I would have followed into any situation without question. These were the folks who could both lead with vision and manage with precision, truly inspiring those around them. Then, there was a sizable group of officers who were great at managing the day-to-day operations but didn't exactly exude the leadership qualities that inspire others. They could keep things running smoothly, but leading? Not so much. And finally, there was the unfortunate group of officers who were neither good leaders nor good managers. They struggled to command respect or even keep things organized, making every task feel like a march uphill with a heavy rucksack. It was a stark reminder that while management skills can be taught, true leadership is something much harder to pin down— and no amount of training or rank insignia can create a leader if the essential traits aren't there.

Leadership doesn't magically appear with a shiny bar on your collar, nor does it come bundled with a freshly printed degree in leadership. You can't just pin on a rank or hang a diploma on the wall and suddenly expect people to follow you into the fray. True leadership is about earning respect, inspiring others, and making tough decisions—not about flashing credentials. Whether it's in the military or the world of higher education, the title alone doesn't make you a leader. It's your actions, character, and ability to connect with and motivate others that truly define whether you're someone worth following.

These programs emphasize applied research that directly impacts educational practice and policy, aligning with the needs of community college leaders who must implement and evaluate programs, improve institutional effectiveness, and address real-world educational challenges (Levin, 2001; Osguthorpe & Wong, 1993; Perry, 2016). The applied nature of Ed.D. research equips leaders with the tools to make data-driven decisions and implement best practices in their institutions. Many Ed.D. programs are designed for working professionals who already have significant experience in educational settings, allowing them to continue working while pursuing advanced training in leadership and management (Eddy & VanDerLinden, 2006; Levin, 2001; Shulman et al., 2006).

The Ed.D. often include coursework and training specifically relevant to community college settings, such as community college governance, student affairs, curriculum development, and workforce education (Levin, 2001; Osguthorpe & Wong, 1993; Perry, 2016; Townsend & Twombly, 2007; Shulman et al., 2006). This targeted curriculum helps future leaders understand the unique challenges and opportunities within community colleges, preparing them to effectively lead these institutions.

Community college leaders need practical leadership skills to handle day-to-day operations, strategic planning, and community engagement. Ed.D. programs typically focus on developing these practical skills, whereas Ph.D. programs often emphasize theoretical research, leadership, and academic scholarship (Eddy & VanDerLinden, 2006; Levin, 2001). This practical orientation makes Ed.D. holders well-suited for the hands-on leadership required in community colleges. Individuals pursuing leadership roles in community colleges often have career goals aligned with educational administration rather than academic research. The Ed.D. degree aligns with these career aspirations, providing the knowledge and skills needed to advance in educational leadership roles (Cohen & Brawer, 2008; Perry, 2016; Shulman et al., 2006). In contrast, the Ph.D. degree is more suited for those pursuing careers in academic research and teaching at four-year universities.

Comparing Ed.D. (Doctor of Education) programs with Ph.D. (Doctor of Philosophy) programs involves considering their focus, rigor, and intended outcomes. Ed.D. programs emphasize applying research to practice, focusing on leadership, administration, and practical problem-solving in educational settings (Eddy & VanDerLinden, 2006). These programs often cater to working professionals with flexible part-time and online options. In contrast, Ph.D. programs focus on original research, theoretical foundations, complex problem-solving skills, leadership, and independent thinking. The Ph.D. requires extensive coursework in research methodologies, leadership, comprehensive exams, and a dissertation contributing new knowledge to the field, often taking longer to complete (4-7 years) compared to Ed.D. programs (2-3 years).

Leadership and Career Advancement in Community Colleges

Leaders in community colleges often prioritize advancing their careers due to several underlying factors. The culture within two-year higher education systems emphasizes career progression and professional development, pressuring leaders to seek higher positions, prestigious titles, or opportunities at larger institutions to demonstrate success and ambition (Eddy & VanDerLinden, 2006; Russell, 2024; Markkula Center for Applied Ethics, 2024; ERIC, 2024, Collaborative Universities, 2024).

Studies have shown that community college leaders prioritize career advancement over their current roles due to the higher education culture's emphasis on progression and the significant challenges they face, such as limited resources and bureaucratic obstacles (Cohen & Brawer, 2008; Levin, 2001). The demanding nature of their positions and the instability within community colleges drive them to seek more stable and supportive opportunities. Additionally, professional development opportunities and personal ambitions motivate these leaders to pursue higher-status and broader-impact roles (Russell, 2024; Markkula Center for Applied Ethics, 2024; ERIC, 2024, Collaborative Universities, 2024).

"Everything rises and falls on leadership" ~*John Maxwell*

The instability of policies, funding, and governance within community colleges can create an environment where leaders feel the need to move on to more stable or predictable positions to achieve their long-term career goals. Many leaders aspire to have a broader impact on the education system, and moving to a higher position or a different institution can provide a larger platform to influence policies, practices, and innovations in higher education (Russell, 2024; Markkula Center for Applied Ethics, 2024; ERIC, 2024, Collaborative Universities, 2024). Personal ambitions, such as achieving higher status, increased compensation, and greater influence, also motivate leaders to focus on career advancement (Russell, 2024; ERIC, 2024). Leadership roles at larger or more prestigious institutions are often seen as more desirable and are associated with higher recognition and prestige, attracting community college leaders to pursue opportunities that offer these perceived benefits (Russell, 2024; Markkula Center for Applied Ethics, 2024; ERIC, 2024, Collaborative Universities, 2024). Understanding these dynamics is essential for developing strategies to support leaders in their current roles and retain talented individuals within the community college system.

Would-be leaders in community colleges often claim that effective leadership is all about strategic planning, data-driven decision-making, and a mix of transformational, collaborative, and servant leadership styles. It sounds impressive, right? But let's be honest—many of them are more likely to rely on anecdotal statements than actual data when making decisions. They throw around the latest fashionable buzzwords to sound smart, but when it comes down to it, they're often just going with their personal career goals or repeating what they've heard from other wood-be leaders. Instead of truly leveraging data to drive outcomes, these would-be leaders are often just playing their part, hoping no one notices that the "data-driven decisions" they boast about are more about sounding savvy than being genuinely strategic.

Nepotism in Community College Leadership

Nepotism runs rampant in the American community Colleges across the United States. This is the practice of favoring relatives or friends for jobs and other opportunities, significantly impacting community college leadership. In this context, nepotism manifests in various ways, from hiring practices to allocating resources and career advancement opportunities that favor their relatives or friends. Relatives and friends of existing staff or administrators receive preferential treatment during the hiring process, leading to positions being filled based on connections rather than qualifications or merit, undermining the transparency and fairness of recruitment processes (Smith, 2019). Leaders tend to allocate resources, such as funding, facilities, or professional development opportunities, in a way that disproportionately benefits their relatives or friends, skewing the institution's priorities and potentially diverting resources away from areas of greatest need (Johnson & Lee, 2020). This also is found with promotion practices, where relatives or friends of leaders are promoted more rapidly or frequently than other employees, regardless of performance or qualifications, leading to a decrease in overall employee morale and motivation (Adams, 2018).

"If you are a non-producer in a leadership position you will produce more non-producers." ~John C Maxwell

Nepotism also creates conflicts of interest, where decisions are made based on personal relationships rather than what is best for the college, and friends and relatives in leadership positions are less likely to be held accountable for poor performance or misconduct, further undermining institutional integrity (Thompson, 2021). Additionally, many educational institutions have policies against nepotism to promote fairness and equality, and violating these policies can lead to legal and ethical ramifications, however, these policies are ignored for career gain. Perceptions of nepotism can damage the reputation of a community college, leading to decreased trust and confidence among stakeholders, including students, faculty, and the broader community (Miller, 2022). Addressing nepotism in community college leadership requires clear policies, enforcement of those policies, transparent practices, and a commitment to fairness and equity. Community colleges must actively work to create an environment where hiring, resource allocation, and promotions are based on merit and qualifications, not your friend network, to ensure that all employees have equal opportunities to succeed (Davis, 2017).

"The very essence of leadership is that you have to have vision. You can't blow an uncertain trumpet." ~Theodore M. Hesburgh

Community College Faculty

The hardworking faculty at community colleges are the backbone of these institutions, dedicated to providing quality education and support to a diverse student body. Many educators hold degrees from top-rated institutions and choose to teach at community colleges because of their passion for teaching over research (Cohen, Brawer, & Kisker, 2014). Despite facing challenges such as limited resources, high teaching loads, and the need for continuous professional development, they remain committed to their students' success (Levin, Kater, & Wagoner, 2006). These faculty members often go above and beyond by offering personalized attention, mentoring, and advising, helping students navigate their educational and career paths. They also play a crucial role in developing innovative curricula that align with local workforce needs, ensuring that students acquire relevant skills and knowledge (Grubb & Gabriner, 2013). Their dedication and resilience are instrumental in fostering an inclusive and supportive learning environment, ultimately contributing to the mission of community colleges to promote social mobility and economic growth (Townsend & Twombly, 2007).

"The greatest leaders mobilize others by coalescing people around a shared vision."
~Ken Blanchard

However, there is a notable contrast between those faculty members who view teaching as their primary career and those who treat their teaching roles as a source of passive income while moonlighting in other jobs. While student success is frequently emphasized, apparently treating teaching as a side hustle doesn't exactly contribute to that success. The latter group often approaches their positions with the mindset of "how little can I do and still get paid?" minimizing their effort in course preparation, student engagement, and grading. Their primary attention often shifts to their other ventures, such as roles in private industry, consulting, or freelance work, making them about as available as a unicorn at a petting zoo. They cherry-pick the most convenient teaching assignments to fit around their main gigs, opting for courses with fewer demands or more convenient hours. Consequently, their interaction with students can become as engaging as watching paint dry, focusing primarily on delivering lectures or assignments with the absolute minimum effort. This stellar approach can boost the quality of education and support provided to students, right? It also does wonders for the faculty's involvement in college activities and professional development. So, while this might work great for their bank accounts, it doesn't quite support student success, leaving students yearning for the kind of faculty engagement that extends beyond the lecture hall.

"A genuine leader is not a searcher for consensus but a molder of consensus"
~Dr. M.L. King

A typical community college faculty work schedule involves a variety of responsibilities. Faculty members usually teach 15 credit hours per semester, equating to about 4 to 5 classes. In addition to class hours, they hold office hours for student consultations, typically around 5 to 10 hours per week. Significant time is also dedicated to preparing lectures, creating exams, grading assignments, and updating course materials. Faculty members attend departmental, committee, and faculty meetings, and often provide academic advising to help students with course selection and educational planning. Professional development is also a key component, with faculty participating in conferences, workshops, and sometimes engaging in research and publications. Other duties include curriculum development and community service or outreach programs. Overall, a faculty member's weekly schedule generally involves 35-40 hours on campus, with additional time spent on class preparation, grading, and other responsibilities outside of official hours.

"A good leader takes a little more than his share of the blame, a little less than his share of the credit." ~Arnold Glasow

On the other hand, some community college faculty members, often considered poor quality by their peers and students, work only 15 hours per week. These individuals typically focus solely on their teaching responsibilities, often because they hold other jobs outside of the college. They may teach the required number of classes, but their commitment to the role is limited, treating their faculty position as a source of passive income. As a result, they might spend minimal time on campus beyond their teaching hours, neglecting office hours, student consultations, and other academic responsibilities. Their involvement in curriculum development, departmental meetings, and professional development activities is often minimal, leading to a perception of disengagement and lack of dedication to their primary faculty role. This behavior is reflected upon all faculty and not just the passive income faculty.

"Leadership is not about being in charge. It is about taking care of those in your charge" ~ Jocko Willink and Leif Babin

Chapter 5

Beyond Grades: Holistic Student Success

S tudent success is the primary goal for community colleges, extending beyond academic achievements to encompass a broad spectrum of outcomes. At its core, student success involves attaining educational goals, such as completing degrees or certificates. It also includes personal development, acquiring critical thinking and problem-solving skills, and preparing for career and life beyond school (Kuh, Kinzie, Buckley, Bridges, & Hayek, 2006). Elements defining student success include academic achievement, graduation and retention rates, skill development, career readiness, personal growth, and civic engagement. Academic achievement includes grades, test scores, and other performance measures. Graduation and retention rates reflect program completion and year-to-year persistence. Skill development covers critical thinking, communication, and collaboration. Career readiness involves acquiring job skills and securing employment in the field of study. Personal growth encompasses self-awareness, resilience, and the ability to navigate life's challenges. Civic engagement includes community service and activities contributing to the greater good (Tinto, 2012).

The hardworking faculty at community colleges are the backbone of these institutions, dedicated to providing quality education and support to a diverse student body. Many of these educators hold degrees from top-rated institutions and choose to teach at community colleges because of their passion for teaching over research (Cohen,

Brawer, & Kisker, 2014). Despite facing challenges such as limited resources, high teaching loads, and the need for continuous professional development, they remain committed to their students' success (Levin, Kater, & Wagoner, 2006). These faculty members often go above and beyond by offering personalized attention, mentoring, and advising, helping students navigate their educational and career paths. They also play a crucial role in developing innovative curricula that align with local workforce needs, ensuring that students acquire relevant skills and knowledge (Grubb & Gabriner, 2013). Their dedication and resilience are instrumental in fostering an inclusive and supportive learning environment, ultimately contributing to the mission of community colleges to promote social mobility and economic growth (Townsend & Twombly, 2007).

"With the changing economy, no one has lifetime employment. But community colleges provide lifetime employability" ~Barack Obama

However, there is a notable contrast between those faculty members who view teaching as their primary career and those who treat their teaching roles as a source of passive income while engaging in other jobs. While student success is frequently emphasized, treating the teaching role as passive income does not contribute to student success. The latter group often approaches their positions with a different mindset, minimizing their effort in course preparation, student engagement, and grading. Their primary attention often shifts to their other jobs or ventures, such as roles in private industry, consulting, or freelance work, leading to limited availability and responsiveness to both students and colleagues. They might choose teaching assignments that offer the most flexibility to accommodate their main careers, selecting courses with fewer demands or more convenient hours. Consequently, their interaction with students can become less intensive, focusing primarily on delivering lectures or assignments with minimal additional engagement. This approach can impact the quality of education and support provided to students, as well as diminish the faculty's involvement in college activities and professional development.

Metrics and Indicators of Success

To effectively measure student success, various metrics and indicators are employed, providing a comprehensive view of a student's educational journey. Key metrics include academic performance, graduation and retention rates, post-graduation outcomes, skill acquisition and development, student engagement and satisfaction, and personal and social development. Academic performance is measured through grades, GPA, and standardized test scores. Graduation and retention rates indicate program completion and continuity in studies (Astin, 1993). Post-graduation outcomes include employment rates in the field of study and graduate school enrollment.

Skill acquisition and development are assessed through internships, co-ops, and competency evaluations. Student engagement and satisfaction are gauged through surveys and feedback on extracurricular activities such as clubs and organizations (Pascarella & Terenzini, 2005). Personal and social development is measured through self-assessment tools evaluating emotional intelligence and resilience and community involvement in volunteer work and civic activities. These metrics provide a holistic view of student success, recognizing it as a combination of academic performance, skills, and personal growth (Kuh et al., 2006).

"The beautiful thing about learning is that no one can take it away from you."
~B.B. King

Programs and Initiatives for Student Success

Programs and initiatives aimed at enhancing student success are diverse, targeting various aspects of the student experience to foster academic achievement, personal growth, and career readiness. Examples include first-year experience programs offering orientation, mentorship, and academic advising (Upcraft, Gardner, & Barefoot, 2005). Learning communities, where students take a set of courses together, foster community and academic collaboration (Tinto, 2003). Early alert systems identify students at risk of academic failure and provide timely interventions. Programs supporting underrepresented and marginalized student populations, such as TRIO programs, promote inclusivity and ensure all students have the opportunity to succeed (Perna, 2005).

Academic Support Services

Academic support services are essential for student success strategies, offering resources to help students achieve their academic goals. These services include tutoring centers for subject-specific help and writing centers for writing and research skills (Gordon, Habley, &

Grites, 2008). Academic advising guides course selection, degree requirements, and academic planning. Supplemental instruction, peer-led study sessions, reinforces key concepts and promotes collaborative learning (Arendale, 2004). Workshops on time management, study skills, and exam preparation equip students with tools for academic success.

Career Counseling and Job Placement

Career counseling and job placement services prepare students for life after graduation, helping them transition from college to the workforce. Career counseling offers individual and group sessions to explore career options, assess skills and interests, and develop career plans (Niles & Harris-Bowlsbey, 2013). Job placement services assist students in finding employment opportunities related to their field of study through partnerships with local businesses and industries. These services include resume and cover letter writing assistance, interview preparation, and job search strategies. Career centers often host job fairs, networking events, and professional development workshops on topics like building a professional online presence and negotiating job offers (Kuh, Kinzie, Schuh, & Whitt, 2010).

Academic Advising

Centralized student advising in community colleges aims to streamline the advising process by creating a uniform system where students receive consistent information and guidance from a centralized office or set of advisors. However, this approach often falls short in addressing the diverse and individualized needs of community college students. A significant issue with centralized advising is the lack of personalized attention. Community college students come from varied backgrounds, including non-traditional students, working adults, first-generation college students, and those requiring remedial education. A one-size-fits-all advising model fails to consider these unique circumstances, leading to generic advice that does not adequately support each student's specific educational and career goals. This impersonal approach can result in students feeling misunderstood and unsupported, ultimately affecting their academic performance and persistence.

Moreover, centralized advising systems can become overburdened due to high student-to-advisor ratios, leading to long wait times and rushed advising sessions. Advisors, inundated with a large caseload, may not have the time to build meaningful relationships with their advisees or fully understand their situations. This can lead to miscommunication, overlooked details, and generic advice that fails to address critical issues like transfer requirements, financial aid opportunities, and academic challenges. Furthermore, the centralized model often lacks the flexibility to adapt to the evolving needs of students throughout their academic journey. As students' progress, their advising needs become more complex and specialized, requiring a more tailored approach that a centralized system is ill-equipped to provide. These shortcomings highlight the need for a more decentralized and personalized advising model that can better support the diverse and dynamic student population in community colleges.

Case Studies of Successful Programs

Successful programs designed to enhance student success often share common characteristics, such as comprehensive support services, strong community engagement, and data-driven strategies. One notable example is the City University of New York's (CUNY) Accelerated Study in Associate Programs (ASAP). This program aims to increase the graduation rates of community college students by providing a range of supports, including tuition waivers, free textbooks, and transportation assistance. Additionally, students receive intensive advising, career counseling, and tutoring. Research has shown that ASAP nearly doubles the graduation rates of participating students compared to non-participants (Scrivener et al., 2015).

Another exemplary program is Georgia State University's Panther Retention Grant initiative, which identifies students at risk of dropping out due to financial difficulties and provides them with small, targeted grants. This program has been highly effective in reducing dropout rates and helping students stay on track to graduate. Furthermore, Georgia State's use of predictive analytics to identify students who need academic support has significantly improved their retention and graduation rates (Renick, 2019).

Examples of High-Performing Community Colleges

Several community colleges have demonstrated exceptional performance in terms of student success. Valencia College in Florida is often cited as a model for its comprehensive approach to student support. Valencia's Learning Support Centers provide extensive tutoring and academic resources, and the college's New Student Experience program helps students transition to college life with personalized advising and career planning. As a result, Valencia has consistently high graduation and transfer rates (Jenkins & Kerrigan, 2008).

A noteworthy high-performing institution is Montgomery College in Maryland, which has earned recognition for its innovative programs aimed at closing achievement gaps. The Achieving the Promise Academy at Montgomery College offers coaching, mentoring, and academic support to underrepresented students, leading to significant improvements in their academic performance and retention rates. Additionally, the college's emphasis on partnerships with local businesses and industries enhances students' career readiness and job placement outcomes (Bailey, Jaggars, & Jenkins, 2015).

"Education is the most powerful weapon you can use to change the world."
~B.B. King

Success Stories of Individual Students

Success stories of individual students often highlight the transformative impact of supportive programs and initiatives. For instance, consider the story of Maria, a first-generation college student at a community college participating in the ASAP program. Maria struggled initially with balancing work, family responsibilities, and her studies. However, with the support of ASAP's academic advising, financial assistance, and tutoring services, she excelled academically and graduated with honors. Maria's success story underscores the importance of comprehensive support systems in helping students overcome challenges and achieve their educational goals (Scrivener et al., 2015).

Another inspiring example is John, a student at Georgia State University who faced financial difficulties that threatened his ability to stay enrolled. Through the Panther Retention Grant initiative, John received a small grant that allowed him to pay his tuition and continue his studies. With the additional support of career counseling and academic advising, John graduated on time and secured a job in his field of study shortly after graduation. His story illustrates how targeted financial aid and personalized support can make a critical difference in student outcomes (Renick, 2019).

Transferability of Community College Credits to Universities

The transferability of credits between community colleges and universities presents several challenges that can affect students' academic progress, financial stability, and overall educational experience. These issues can impede the seamless transition from a two-year institution to a four-year institution, potentially delaying graduation and increasing costs (American Association of Community Colleges, 2021; Bailey et al., 2005; 2015; Cohen et al., 2014). Understanding these challenges is crucial for developing effective solutions and policies to support transfer students. Moreover, the connectivity between the community college and university needs to be made more solid for a true seamless transfer of credits, and the courses a student is taking are part of the university program.

Inconsistent Credit Recognition

One of the primary issues with transferability is the inconsistent recognition of credits earned at community colleges by four-year universities. Not all credits transfer equally, and some courses taken at community colleges may not meet the specific requirements of a university's degree programs (American Association of Community Colleges, 2021; Bailey et al., 2005; 2015; Cohen et al., 2014). This inconsistency can result in students having to retake courses they have already completed, leading to wasted time and resources. Different institutions may have varying standards for what constitutes an equivalent course, creating barriers for students who assume their credits will automatically transfer.

Lack of Articulation Agreements

Articulation agreements are formal agreements between community colleges and universities that outline the transfer policies for specific programs and courses. A lack of these agreements can create uncertainty for students about which credits will transfer and how they will be applied toward their degree (American Association of Community Colleges, 2021; Bailey et al., 2005; 2015; Cohen et al., 2014). Without clear articulation agreements, students may struggle to plan their course schedules effectively, potentially taking courses that do not contribute to their intended degree at the university level.

Transfer and Articulation Failures

Community college credit transfer and articulation issues significantly impact students' educational pathways. Credit transfer involves transferring credits earned at a community college to a four-year institution, ideally having those credits count towards a degree. However, the transferability of credits can vary widely, with some institutions accepting only a limited number and certain courses not meeting specific degree program requirements (University of California, n.d.). Articulation agreements are formal agreements between community colleges and four-year institutions that outline which courses will transfer and how they apply to degree programs, providing a clear pathway for students (American Association of Community Colleges, 2021). Despite these efforts, issues can arise when courses transfer but do not align with the four-year institution's specific degree requirements. For instance, a student may transfer 60 credits, but only 45 might apply to their major, with the remaining 15 counting as elective credits, leading to longer degree completion times and additional costs.

"The mind is not a vessel to be filled but a fire to be ignited."
~Plutarch

Discrepancies between community college courses and the four-year institution's requirements, even with articulation agreements, can result in some credits not being applicable to a student's major. Changes in curricula or degree requirements at the four-year institution can further complicate the transfer process, making previously agreed-upon credits obsolete or less relevant (American Association of Community Colleges, 2021). In summary, while community college credits can transfer to four-year institutions, they do not always apply directly to a student's intended degree program, often requiring additional coursework and extending the time to graduation.

Misalignment of Curricula

The curricula of community colleges and universities may not always align, particularly in specialized or upper-division courses. This misalignment can create gaps in students' knowledge and preparedness for advanced coursework at the university level (American Association of Community Colleges, 2021; Bailey et al., 2005; 2015; Cohen et al., 2014). For example, a course in organic chemistry at a community college may not cover the same depth or range of topics as the equivalent course at a university, leaving transfer students at a disadvantage when they continue their studies.

"A person who never made a mistake never tried anything new."
~Albert Einstein

Limited Advising and Support

Effective academic advising is critical for helping students navigate the transfer process, but many community colleges face resource constraints that limit the availability of advising services. Inadequate advising can lead to students taking unnecessary courses or missing prerequisites needed for their intended major at a four-year institution (American Association of Community Colleges, 2021; Bailey et al., 2005; 2015; Cohen et al., 2014). Additionally, students may not receive adequate guidance on selecting a university that aligns with their academic and career goals, further complicating the transfer process.

Financial Implications

Students face significant financial challenges related to the transferability of credits and courses. If students must retake courses or take additional courses to meet university requirements, this can increase the overall cost of their education. Additionally, differences in tuition rates between community colleges and universities can result in unexpected financial burdens for transfer students (American Association of Community Colleges, 2021; Bailey et al., 2005; 2015; Cohen et al., 2014). Scholarships and financial aid packages may also be affected by the transfer process, creating further financial uncertainty. Nonetheless, students who transfer to a university tend to lose significant money in credit loss as shown in the below table.

The Disenfranchisement of Community College Students

The disenfranchisement of a community college student who transfers to a university and realizes they must make up significant credits due to a failure of credit transfer and articulation is a profound and disheartening experience. This situation often begins with the student's hope and ambition, believing that their time and effort spent at the community college will seamlessly transition into their pursuit of a bachelor's degree. However, upon transferring, they are confronted with the harsh reality that many of their credits are not accepted as equivalent or are only counted as electives, which do not advance their progress toward their major (University of California, n.d.).

This realization can lead to a profound sense of frustration and disillusionment. The student feels misled by the initial assurances that their community college coursework would be adequately recognized (American Association of Community Colleges, 2021). The financial burden increases as they must pay for additional semesters and courses that they believed they had already completed. The time investment is also significant, as they find themselves having to repeat courses or take additional ones, delaying their graduation and entry into the workforce.

The emotional impact is equally severe. The student may experience a sense of failure and question the value of their community college education. This feeling of being undervalued and unsupported can erode their confidence and motivation. The bureaucratic challenges and the need to navigate complex academic requirements further add to their disenfranchisement. The entire experience underscores a systemic issue within higher education, where the lack of effective credit transfer and articulation agreements undermines the goals and achievements of community college students, leaving them feeling marginalized and disheartened in their academic journey (American Association of Community Colleges, 2021).

State	Average Credits Lost	Cost of Credits Lost in $
California	12	4200
Texas	15	5250
Florida	10	3500
New York	13	4550
Illinois	14	4900
Pennsylvania	12	4200
Ohio	11	3850
Georgia	16	5600
N. Carolina	15	5250
Michigan	10	3500
Nevada	13	4550

Sources: National Student Clearinghouse Research Center (2020); Community College Research Center (CCRC) at Teachers College, Columbia University (2015); State Higher Education Executive Officers Association (SHEEO, 2018); U.S. Department of Education, National Center for Education Statistics (NCES, 2019)

Institutional Policies and Bureaucracy

The bureaucratic processes involved in transferring credits can be complex and time-consuming. Different institutions have their own policies and procedures for evaluating transfer credits, which can create delays and confusion for students (American Association of Community Colleges, 2021; Bailey et al., 2005; Cohen et al., 2014). The lack of standardized processes across institutions exacerbates these issues, making it difficult for students to understand and navigate transfer requirements.

"Never let the fear of striking out stop you from playing the game."
~Babe Ruth

Accreditation and Quality Concerns

The accreditation status and perceived quality of community colleges can influence the acceptance of transfer credits by universities. Some universities may be hesitant to accept credits from institutions they perceive as having lower academic standards (American Association of Community Colleges, 2021; Bailey et al., 2005; Cohen et al., 2014). This creates barriers for students transferring from community colleges to more selective or prestigious universities. Ensuring that community colleges maintain high academic standards and are accredited by recognized accrediting bodies is essential for facilitating credit transfer.

Efforts to Improve Transferability

Community colleges face several challenges regarding the transferability of credits, impacting students' educational progress and costs. Inconsistent credit recognition between institutions, variations in curriculum, and a lack of formal articulation agreements often result in lost credit during transfer. Differences in course levels and accreditation issues further complicate this process. Additionally, limited advising resources at community colleges hinder students' understanding of transfer requirements, while frequent changes in university policies can invalidate previously accepted credits. Course content differences and varying state policies also pose significant hurdles, compounded by the "perception" that community college courses are of lower quality than those at four-year institutions. Addressing these challenges requires developing strong articulation agreements, standardizing curricula, enhancing advising services, advocating for statewide and cross-border transfer policies, and maintaining regular communication between institutions to facilitate a smoother transfer process and improve educational outcomes for students.

"Community college is like a disco with books: Here's ten dollars; let me get my learn on!" ~Chris Rock

To address these transferability issues, several initiatives and policies have been implemented (American Association of Community Colleges, 2021; Bailey et al., 2005; Cohen et al., 2014):

- **Statewide Transfer Agreements**: Some states have implemented statewide transfer agreements that guarantee the transfer of credits between public community colleges and universities within the state. These agreements often include a common course numbering system and general education requirements, simplifying the transfer process.

- **Pathway Programs**: Many institutions have developed pathway programs that provide clear and structured transfer pathways for students. These programs outline the specific courses and requirements needed for successful transfer to a four-year institution, reducing uncertainty and improving alignment between curricula.

- **Enhanced Advising Services**: Increasing the availability and quality of academic advising services at community colleges can help students plan their courses more effectively and understand transfer requirements. This support can include transfer fairs, workshops, and dedicated transfer advisors who specialize in helping students navigate the transfer process.

- **Joint Admissions Programs**: Some community colleges and universities offer joint admissions programs, allowing students to be simultaneously admitted to both institutions. These programs provide students with access to resources and advising staff from both institutions, facilitating a smoother transition and better alignment of academic programs.

- **Technology Solutions**: Leveraging technology to create online portals and databases that track and compare course equivalencies can streamline the transfer process. These tools can help students and advisors quickly determine which credits will transfer and how they will apply to different degree programs.

While transferability issues between community colleges and universities present significant challenges, ongoing efforts to develop clear articulation agreements, improve advising services, and align curricula are essential for supporting transfer students. By addressing these issues, institutions can enhance the transfer process, reduce barriers to degree completion, and ensure that students have a seamless and successful educational experience.

In conclusion, the primary issue with student success is credit loss when transferring from community college to a university is the inconsistent and unclear transfer policies that vary widely between institutions and even departments. This inconsistency, coupled with poor communication and administrative hurdles, results in students often losing credits, leading to repeated courses, extended graduation timelines, and increased financial burdens. Addressing these challenges requires improved articulation agreements, standardized transfer policies, and better support for transfer students to ensure a seamless and efficient transition from community colleges to universities.

Failure is not an option when it comes to educating the masses— after all, no one wants a generation of professional couch potatoes. Our success isn't just a nice-to-have; it's absolutely essential for the future of our students and communities. This highlights the importance of juggling resources and keeping everyone accountable, kind of like herding cats but with diplomas. To keep community colleges thriving, we need to tackle these challenges head-on, unleash our inner innovators, and maintain a rock-solid commitment to educational excellence.

Integrating Community Colleges into the University System for Seamless Student Success

Integrating community colleges directly into the university system to ensure seamless credit transfer and program alignment involves several strategic actions. First, developing a unified curriculum aligns community college courses directly with university degree requirements, ensuring that all credits earned at the community college level are automatically applicable to the student's chosen degree program (American Association of Community Colleges, 2021). Implementing a standardized 2+2 program structure, where students spend two years at a community college before seamlessly continuing into the third year of a four-year degree program at the university, is crucial (University of California, n.d.). Streamlining administrative processes and systems, such as a shared registration system and unified student records, facilitates smooth transitions for students. Ensuring that advisors from both the community college and university are trained to provide consistent guidance on course selection and transfer requirements is essential.

Fostering collaborative governance by establishing joint governance structures, including representatives from both community colleges and universities, ensures that decision-making processes reflect the needs and perspectives of both types of institutions. Enhancing communication and coordination through regular joint faculty meetings, shared professional development opportunities, and collaborative planning sessions promotes a unified approach. Utilizing integrated technology systems for real-time data sharing helps track student progress and ensures alignment of courses. Predictive analytics can identify potential transfer issues early and address them proactively. Cultivating a unified institutional culture emphasizes the shared mission of student success, highlighting the benefits of a seamless educational pathway. Recognizing and rewarding efforts by faculty and staff who contribute to improving transfer processes and enhancing cooperation within the integrated system is important. By integrating community colleges as part of the university system, institutions can create a more cohesive higher education experience, ensuring that credits transfer smoothly, programs are synchronized, and students can achieve their educational goals without unnecessary delays or financial burdens.

Integrating community colleges directly into the university system for a smooth transition is like trying to get your cat to take a bath: it's messy, it requires a lot of patience, and there's a good chance you'll end up drenched. But fear not—if done right, it can be smoother than a catnip high.

First off, we need to make sure community college courses and university degree requirements are as in sync as peanut butter and jelly. No more "Oops, your calculus class doesn't count here" moments. Let's align those curriculums like we're setting up a blind date—match made in academic heaven.

Next, we need a 2+2 program structure that's so seamless, students will think they've accidentally walked into an episode of "The Twilight Zone" where everything just works perfectly. Imagine students spending two years at community college and then sliding into their university degree like it's their favorite pair of sweatpants—easy, comfy, and totally stress-free.

Streamlining administrative processes is key. This means no more filling out forms that feel like they were designed by a sadistic game show host. We need to ditch the paperwork mountain and replace it with a shared registration system that's as intuitive as ordering a pizza online. And let's not forget unified student records—one place where your academic history is as easy to find as your favorite Netflix show.

Advisors need to be in sync too. Imagine having advisors from both institutions trained to give consistent guidance, like having a GPS that actually knows where it's going and doesn't suddenly decide to take you on a scenic route through a cornfield.

Finally, fostering collaborative governance is essential. Think of it as forming an Avengers team, but for education. We need representatives from both community colleges and universities working together to make the transition as smooth as a freshly waxed floor. It's like having your cake and eating it too, but with fewer crumbs and less risk of a sugar high.

In short, integrating community colleges into the university system should be so smooth that students feel like they're on a never-ending academic joyride. With a little creativity, a dash of humor, and a lot of teamwork, we can make sure that students' educational journeys are as seamless as they are successful. After all, we're not just preparing them for the future—we're giving them a front-row seat to the greatest show on earth: their own success story.

Chapter 6

Facing Forward: Challenges and Opportunities for Community Colleges

The bureaucratic processes involved in transferring credits are a breeze—said no student ever. Different institutions each have their own unique maze of policies and procedures for evaluating transfer credits, which naturally creates a delightful experience of delays and confusion for students (American Association of Community Colleges, 2021; Bailey et al., 2005; Cohen et al., 2014). The utter lack of standardized processes across institutions just adds to the fun, making it nearly impossible for students to understand and navigate transfer requirements. Because, of course, who wouldn't want to spend extra time and effort deciphering a bureaucratic nightmare while trying to further their education?

Accreditation and Quality Concerns

The accreditation status and perceived quality of community colleges can influence the acceptance of transfer credits by universities. Some universities may be hesitant to accept credits from institutions they perceive as having lower academic standards (American Association of Community Colleges, 2021; Bailey et al., 2005; Cohen et al., 2014). This creates barriers for students transferring from community colleges to more selective or prestigious universities. Ensuring that community colleges maintain high academic standards and are accredited by recognized accrediting bodies is essential for facilitating credit transfer. Such successful programs look like:

- **Efforts to Improve Transferability:** To address these transferability issues, several initiatives and policies have been implemented (American Association of Community Colleges, 2021; Bailey et al., 2005; Cohen et al., 2014):

- **Statewide Transfer Agreements**: Some states have implemented statewide transfer agreements that guarantee the transfer of credits between public community colleges and universities within the state. These agreements often include a common course numbering system and general education requirements, simplifying the transfer process.

- **Pathway Programs**: Many institutions have developed pathway programs that provide clear and structured transfer pathways for students. These programs outline the specific courses and requirements needed for successful transfer to a four-year institution, reducing uncertainty and improving alignment between curricula.

- **Enhanced Advising Services**: Increasing the availability and quality of academic advising services at community colleges can help students plan their courses more effectively and understand transfer requirements. This support can include transfer fairs, workshops, and dedicated transfer advisors who specialize in helping students navigate the transfer process.

- **Joint Admissions Programs**: Some community colleges and universities offer joint admissions programs, allowing students to be simultaneously admitted to both institutions. These programs provide students with access to resources and advising staff from both institutions, facilitating a smoother transition and better alignment of academic programs.

- **Technology Solutions**: Leveraging technology to create online portals and databases that track and compare course equivalencies can streamline the transfer process. These tools can help students and advisors quickly determine which credits will transfer and how they will apply to different degree programs.

While transferability issues between community colleges and universities present significant challenges, ongoing efforts to develop clear articulation agreements, improve advising services, and align curricula are essential for supporting transfer students. By addressing these issues, institutions can enhance the transfer process, reduce barriers to degree completion, and ensure that students have a seamless and successful educational experience.

Financial Constraints

Community colleges often face significant financial constraints that impact their ability to deliver quality education and support services. These institutions typically rely heavily on state funding, tuition fees, and local government support, all of which can be unpredictable and insufficient to meet the growing needs of their diverse student populations. Budget cuts and limited financial resources can lead to reductions in staff, course offerings, and student services, affecting student retention and success rates (Katsinas, Tollefson, & Reamey, 2008). Additionally, many community colleges struggle to maintain and upgrade their facilities and technology infrastructure due to financial limitations, further hindering their ability to provide a modern and effective learning environment.

Enrollment Fluctuations

Enrollment fluctuations present another major challenge for community colleges. Enrollment numbers can vary significantly, influenced by factors such as economic conditions, demographic changes, and competition from other educational institutions. During economic downturns, community colleges often see an increase in enrollment as individuals seek new skills or credentials to improve their job prospects. Conversely, during periods of economic growth, enrollment may decline as potential students opt to enter the workforce directly (Smith, 2010). This variability makes it difficult for community colleges to plan and allocate resources effectively. Fluctuations in enrollment can also lead to challenges in maintaining a stable faculty and ensuring that course offerings align with student demand.

Impact of COVID-19 on Student Retention

The COVID-19 pandemic has had a profound impact on student retention at community colleges, leading to significant losses in student enrollment. Many community college students come from lower-income backgrounds and work part-time or full-time jobs to support their education. The economic downturn caused by the pandemic resulted in widespread job losses and financial instability, forcing many students to prioritize immediate financial needs over continuing their education, leading to a notable drop in enrollment (Johnson, 2020). Additionally, the abrupt shift to online learning highlighted the digital divide, as many community college students lacked access to reliable internet connections and necessary technology. Without adequate access to online learning platforms, these students faced significant challenges in keeping up with their coursework, leading to increased frustration and dropouts (Smith, 2021).

The transition to remote learning posed numerous academic challenges for both students and faculty. Many students found it difficult to adapt to the new learning environment, which often lacked the interactive and hands-on experiences typical of in-person classes. The lack of engagement, coupled with difficulty accessing academic support services, led to lower academic performance and increased dropout rates (Williams, 2020). Moreover, the pandemic took a toll on mental health, with increased levels of anxiety, stress, and depression among students. Isolation from peers and uncertainty about the future exacerbated these mental health issues, making it difficult for students to stay focused and motivated in their studies, leading to a significant number of students pausing or discontinuing their education (Davis, 2021).

Many community college students are non-traditional students who juggle multiple responsibilities, including work and family obligations. The pandemic intensified these responsibilities, particularly for those caring for sick family members or assisting children with remote schooling. The increased demand on their time and energy made it challenging for many students to continue their education, resulting in higher dropout rates (Miller, 2020). Additionally, uncertainty surrounding the future job market and economic recovery contributed to the decline in student retention. Many students questioned the value of continuing their education amidst such uncertainty, leading them to defer or abandon their studies until the situation stabilizes (Brown, 2020).

Community colleges, already operating with limited resources, faced additional challenges in providing support to students during the pandemic. The strain on resources made it difficult to offer sufficient academic advising, tutoring, and other support services that are critical for student success. The reduced availability of these services further contributed to the decline in student retention (Taylor, 2020). In summary, the COVID-19 pandemic led to a significant loss in student retention at community colleges due to economic hardships, the digital divide, academic challenges, mental health issues, increased responsibilities at home, uncertainty about future prospects, and decreased institutional support. Addressing these issues requires targeted interventions and increased support to help students navigate these unprecedented challenges and continue their education (Lewis, 2012).

Technological Advancements and Online Education

The rapid pace of technological advancements and the growing prevalence of online education present both opportunities and challenges for community colleges. On one hand, technology offers the potential to enhance teaching and learning through digital tools, online resources, and innovative instructional methods. Online education, in particular, provides greater flexibility and accessibility for students who may have work, family, or other commitments that make traditional classroom attendance difficult (Allen & Seaman, 2013). However, integrating technology into the curriculum and expanding online education offerings require significant investment in infrastructure, training, and support services. Many community colleges face challenges in keeping up with these demands due to financial constraints and limited technical expertise.

The shift to online education raises concerns about the quality of instruction and student engagement. Ensuring that online courses are as rigorous and effective as their in-person counterparts requires careful planning, ongoing assessment, and support for both students and faculty. Community colleges must also address the digital divide, as not all students have equal access to the technology and internet connectivity needed to succeed in online courses (Gonzalez, 2020). These challenges necessitate strategic planning and investment to ensure that technological advancements and online education contribute positively to student success.

Opportunities for Growth

Partnerships with industry present a significant opportunity for growth for community colleges. By collaborating with local businesses and industries, community colleges can align their programs with the needs of the job market, ensuring that students acquire relevant skills and are prepared for employment upon graduation. These partnerships can take various forms, including internship programs, apprenticeships, job placement services, and the development of industry-specific training programs (Soares, 2013). For example, many community colleges work with healthcare providers, technology companies, and manufacturing firms to create tailored curricula that meet the specific demands of these sectors. Such collaborations not only enhance the employability of graduates but also provide students with valuable hands-on experience and networking opportunities.

Industry partnerships can also lead to financial support for community colleges through donations, grants, and sponsorships. Businesses may invest in the development of new facilities, such as advanced labs and training centers, which benefit both students and the local economy. These partnerships foster a symbiotic relationship where both the educational institution and the industry partners benefit from shared resources and expertise (Kisker & Carducci, 2003).

Innovation in Curriculum and Delivery

Innovation in curriculum and delivery methods is another area with substantial potential for growth in community colleges. To stay relevant and effective, community colleges must continuously evolve their curricula to reflect changes in technology, industry standards, and educational best practices. This includes integrating emerging technologies such as artificial intelligence, cybersecurity, and data analytics into their programs. Additionally, the adoption of competency-based education models allows students to progress at their own pace and gain credit for prior learning and work experience (Johnstone & Soares, 2014).

Innovative delivery methods, such as blended learning, flipped classrooms, and fully online courses, offer greater flexibility and accessibility for students. Blended learning combines traditional face-to-face instruction with online components, allowing for a more personalized learning experience. Flipped classrooms reverse the traditional teaching model by delivering lecture content online, enabling classroom time to be used for interactive, hands-on activities. Fully online courses provide opportunities for students who may be unable to attend in-person classes due to work or family commitments (Garrison & Kanuka, 2004).

Community colleges can also experiment with micro-credentials and certificate programs that focus on specific skills or competencies. These shorter, more focused programs can quickly respond to the needs of the job market and provide students with tangible credentials that enhance their employability. By embracing these innovations, community colleges can better serve their diverse student populations and improve educational outcomes.

Role of Government Policy

Government policy plays a crucial role in shaping the landscape of community colleges, influencing funding, regulations, and the overall direction of higher education. Federal, state, and local governments each contribute to the development and implementation of policies that impact community colleges. At the federal level, policies such as the Higher Education Act and initiatives like the Pell Grant program provide financial aid and support to low-income students, making higher education more accessible (Thelin, 2011). Additionally, federal grants and funding opportunities, such as those from the Department of Education, help community colleges develop innovative programs and improve infrastructure.

State governments are instrumental in determining the allocation of funding to community colleges through state budgets and appropriations. State policies also influence tuition rates, governance structures, and accountability measures. For example, performance-based funding models, where colleges receive funding based on student outcomes such as graduation rates and job placement, are becoming increasingly common (Dougherty & Reddy, 2013). Local governments can impact community colleges through property taxes and local initiatives that provide additional resources and support for these institutions.

Advocacy Efforts for Community Colleges

Advocacy efforts for community colleges are essential to ensure these institutions receive the support and recognition they need to fulfill their mission. Advocacy can take many forms, including lobbying, public awareness campaigns, and coalition-building. Organizations such as the American Association of Community Colleges (AACC) and the Association of Community College Trustees (ACCT) play a vital role in representing the interests of community colleges at the national level. These organizations work to influence federal and state legislation, secure funding, and promote policies that benefit community colleges and their students (AACC, 2021).

At the state and local levels, community college leaders, faculty, and students often engage in advocacy efforts to highlight the importance of these institutions to policymakers and the public. This can involve meeting with legislators, participating in public hearings, and organizing grassroots campaigns. Effective advocacy highlights the critical role community colleges play in workforce development, economic growth, and providing educational opportunities for diverse populations (Jenkins, 2015).

Advocacy efforts also focus on specific issues such as increasing funding, expanding access to financial aid, and addressing barriers to student success. For example, campaigns to expand eligibility for Pell Grants to cover short-term certificate programs and part-time students have gained traction in recent years. Additionally, advocacy for policies that support student services, such as childcare and transportation, can help address the non-academic barriers that many community college students face (Goldrick-Rab, 2016).

Failure is not an option when it comes to the education of the masses. Our success is essential for the future of our students and communities. Community colleges face significant challenges such as complex credit transfer processes, financial constraints, and fluctuating enrollments, especially in the wake of the COVID-19 pandemic. Ensuring high academic standards and proper accreditation is crucial for overcoming university skepticism and facilitating smooth credit transfers.

Despite these hurdles, there are significant opportunities for growth and relevance in the educational landscape. Initiatives like statewide transfer agreements, pathway programs, enhanced advising services, and joint admissions programs help address transferability challenges. Additionally, technological advancements, industry partnerships, and innovative curriculum delivery methods offer new avenues for community colleges to thrive. Effective resource management and accountability are vital to harness these opportunities and ensure the continued success and growth of community colleges.

Despite the treasure trove of opportunities for growth and relevance in the educational landscape, community colleges often seem to be playing it like a game of "Groundhog Day." Even at my institution, we have all these tools and pathways at our disposal—statewide transfer agreements, enhanced advising services, and magical technological advancements—but we often stick to their old playbook like it's a well-worn security blanket. It's as if the new opportunities are there, waving enthusiastically, but the colleges are like, "Nah, we're good with our tried-and-true routine." So, while there's a world of innovation and partnership waiting to be embraced, community colleges sometimes prefer to keep things just as they are, proving that old habits die hard—even when there's a shiny new roadmap to success just begging to be used.

Chapter 7

Overcoming the Odds: Tackling Community College Student Challenges

C ommunity college students often face a combination of financial, academic, personal, and institutional challenges that contribute to low completion rates and significant debt burdens. Financial constraints are a major issue, as financial aid packages often fail to cover the full cost of attendance, including tuition, fees, books, and living expenses. This shortfall forces many students to take out loans, adding to their debt burden (Goldrick-Rab, 2016). Unexpected expenses such as medical bills, car repairs, or other emergencies can further strain their finances, potentially forcing students to either take on more debt or drop out to manage these expenses (Katsinas, Tollefson, & Reamey, 2008). To afford their education, many students must work long hours, which can interfere with their studies and prolong the time needed to complete their degrees (Smith, 2010).

Academic preparedness is another critical factor, with a significant proportion of community college students required to take remedial courses in subjects like math and English. These courses do not count towards their degree, extending the time and cost of their education (Bailey, Jaggars, & Jenkins, 2015). Additionally, limited access to academic advising, tutoring, and other support services can hinder students' academic progress and success (Karp, 2011).

Personal challenges also play a significant role. Many community college students juggle multiple responsibilities, including work, family, and education. The stress of balancing these responsibilities can negatively impact their academic performance and persistence. Furthermore, the lack of a supportive learning environment, coupled with feelings of isolation, can lead to disengagement and dropout (Smith, 2010).

Comparison of Completion and Graduation Rates
Community Colleges vs. Universities Across U.S. States

State	CC Completion Rate (%)	CC Graduation Rate (%)	University Completion Rate (%)	University Graduation Rate (%)
California	30.5	25.4	65.3	60.2
Texas	29.7	24.8	62.7	58.5
Florida	31.2	26.3	64.8	59.7
New York	32.4	27.1	66.1	61.3
Illinois	28.6	23.7	63.2	58.9
Pennsylvania	27.9	22.9	61.4	57.2
Ohio	29.3	24.3	62.5	58.4
Georgia	30.8	25.7	63.7	59.1
N. Carolina	31.5	26.4	64.3	60.0
Michigan	28.1	23.4	62.1	57.9
Nevada	29.1	24.0	61.8	57.6

NOTE: Completion at the CC includes certificates and associate's degrees.

Institutional barriers, such as complex administrative processes and inadequate support services, also impede student success. Navigating the financial aid system, enrolling in the right courses, and accessing necessary resources can be daunting for many students. Community colleges must address these systemic issues to improve completion rates and reduce student debt burdens.

To effectively support community college students and improve completion rates, it is crucial to understand and address these multifaceted challenges. Implementing comprehensive support systems, enhancing academic preparedness, providing financial assistance, and creating a supportive institutional environment are essential steps toward achieving this goal.

Understanding the Challenges Facing Community College Students

Personal and family obligations further complicate the situation for many community college students. Balancing school with jobs, childcare, and family responsibilities makes it difficult to maintain a full-time course load and remain focused on studies (Goldrick-Rab, 2016). Consequently, many students attend part-time, extending the time needed to complete a degree and increasing the likelihood of dropping out (Smith, 2010).

Institutional barriers also play a significant role. Limited course offerings and scheduling conflicts can delay students' progress. Essential courses might be unavailable or offered at inconvenient times, forcing students to prolong their studies (Karp, 2011). Students planning to transfer to four-year institutions often face difficulties ensuring their credits will transfer. Misalignment of curricula can lead to wasted credits and the need to retake courses, increasing both time and costs (Bailey, Jaggars, & Jenkins, 2015).

Systemic issues, such as inadequate counseling and guidance on course selection, career planning, and financial management, further exacerbate these challenges, leading to poor decision-making that can prolong education and increase debt (Goldrick-Rab, 2016). When students drop out without completing their degrees, they still carry the debt they have accumulated but without the improved earning potential that a degree would provide, making it harder to repay their loans. This combination of challenges creates a cycle where community college students struggle to complete their degrees in a timely manner, if at all, while accruing significant debt, trapping many in financial hardship.

Addressing these issues requires comprehensive support systems, improved financial aid, better academic advising, and more flexible course offerings to help students successfully navigate their educational journey. The multitude of financial, academic, personal, and institutional challenges facing community college students creates significant barriers to degree completion and financial stability. These obstacles, from insufficient financial aid and unexpected expenses to inadequate academic preparation and limited institutional support, collectively hinder students' progress and exacerbate their debt burdens.

Fixing these issues requires a recipe with a little bit of everything: a sprinkle of enhanced financial aid, a dash of robust academic and career advising, a pinch of flexible course offerings, and a heaping spoonful of comprehensive support services tailored to the diverse needs of community college students. By whipping up this concoction, community colleges can better support their students in reaching their educational goals and boosting their long-term financial well-being.

The result? A more equitable and effective higher education system that actually works, because who doesn't love a happy ending?

Chapter 8

Charting the Future: Community College Trends and Predictions

C ommunity colleges are on the brink of significant transformations, driven by evolving educational trends and societal needs. Imagine a world where your local community college isn't just about remedial math but is the epicenter of workforce development, churning out skilled workers faster than you can say "job market." We're talking about an increased emphasis on workforce development, where students graduate with the skills to jump straight into a career without breaking a sweat. Then there's the technological integration—think less chalk and talk, more virtual reality classrooms where dissecting a frog doesn't involve any actual frogs. And let's not forget equity and access, because it's high time everyone gets a fair shot at education, whether you're a single mom, a returning vet, or just someone who took a gap decade. Lastly, lifelong learning will take center stage, turning your local community college into a Hogwarts for the newly graduated high schooler and adults, where education doesn't stop at graduation but continues to enchant and enlighten throughout your life.

Workforce Development

Community colleges are increasingly critical in workforce development, providing training and education aligned with local and regional economic needs. Partnerships with industries will grow, creating tailored training programs for high-demand jobs in healthcare, information technology, advanced manufacturing, and renewable energy (Carnevale, Smith, & Strohl, 2013).

Technology Integration

The integration of technology into education will continue to expand, leveraging online learning platforms, artificial intelligence, and virtual reality to enhance the learning experience. Hybrid and fully online courses will become more prevalent, offering greater flexibility for students. Additionally, data analytics will become more sophisticated, helping improve retention and graduation rates (Means, Bakia, & Murphy, 2014).

Focus on Equity and Access

Ensuring equitable access to education will remain a top priority. Community colleges will continue developing programs and initiatives supporting underrepresented and marginalized student populations. This includes expanding financial aid, providing comprehensive student support services, and addressing barriers to education such as childcare, transportation, and food insecurity (Goldrick-Rab, 2016).

Lifelong Learning

As the job market evolves and the demand for continuous skill development increases, community colleges will play a crucial role in providing lifelong learning opportunities. This includes offering short-term certificates, professional development courses, and continuing education programs that allow individuals to upskill and reskill throughout their careers (Selingo, 2016).

Predictions for Community Colleges

Community colleges are expected to see a significant increase in enrollment as the need for affordable, accessible education grows. This surge will encompass traditional students, such as recent high school graduates, and a diverse array of non-traditional students (Bailey et al., 2015). These non-traditional students include adult learners, part-time students balancing studies with work or family responsibilities, and individuals seeking career changes.

This trend towards greater diversity will see community colleges reflecting broader societal demographic changes. Enrollment among minority students, first-generation college students, and those from low-income backgrounds will increase as community colleges become a viable path to higher education and improved economic prospects

(Bailey et al., 2015). The flexibility offered by community colleges, including evening, weekend, and online classes, will attract students who need adaptable schedules.

The influx of diverse student groups will necessitate adopting more inclusive and supportive educational practices. This means expanding student services such as academic advising, tutoring, childcare, and financial aid to accommodate the unique needs of a heterogeneous student body. By doing so, community colleges can better fulfill their mission of providing equitable and accessible education, fostering a more educated and skilled workforce that meets the economy's evolving demands (Bailey et al., 2015).

Enhanced Partnerships

Collaborations between community colleges, K-12 schools, universities, and industry partners will become more robust, facilitating seamless pathways for students to transition from high school to college and from college to the workforce. Dual enrollment programs will allow high school students to take college courses and earn college credits while still in high school, giving them a head start on their college education and increasing their readiness for higher education (Soares, 2013). Articulation agreements between high schools, community colleges, and universities will outline clear pathways for students to transfer credits seamlessly from one institution to another. These agreements ensure that courses taken at one level of education meet the requirements for the next, preventing redundant coursework and reducing barriers to degree completion (Soares, 2013).

Apprenticeships and partnerships with industry will play a crucial role in bridging the gap between education and the workforce. These programs will offer students hands-on experience in their chosen fields, allowing them to apply classroom learning to real-world situations. Industry partners can provide valuable insights into the skills and knowledge needed in the workforce, helping to shape relevant and up-to-date curricula. Apprenticeships can also lead to direct employment opportunities upon completion, giving students a clear pathway from education to employment. Ongoing collaboration between K-12 schools, community colleges, universities, and industry partners will ensure that educational programs align with student needs and workforce demands. This includes regular communication and planning to update curricula, share resources, and provide support services such as advising, tutoring, and career counseling, creating a more supportive and integrated education system (Soares, 2013).

Financial Sustainability

Community colleges will explore new funding models to ensure financial sustainability. This may include advocating for increased public funding by demonstrating the value and impact of community colleges on local economies and workforce development. Securing more public funds can help mitigate the financial challenges these institutions face and enable them to keep tuition affordable for students. Additionally, developing private sector partnerships can provide community colleges with alternative revenue streams. These partnerships might involve collaborations with local businesses and industries that can offer funding, resources, and real-world learning opportunities for students. By aligning educational programs with the job market's needs, community colleges can attract investment from private companies looking to cultivate a skilled workforce (Katsinas, Tollefson, & Reamey, 2008).

Implementing innovative tuition models such as income share agreements (ISAs) can also play a crucial role in ensuring financial health. ISAs allow students to pay for their education through a percentage of their future income over a fixed period, reducing the immediate financial burden and making college more accessible. This model aligns the success of the institution with the success of its graduates, creating a sustainable funding mechanism. Ensuring financial health will be crucial for maintaining and expanding programs and services, which directly benefit students and the broader community. With stable and diverse funding sources, community colleges can invest in advanced facilities, technology, faculty development, and student support services, enhancing the overall educational experience and outcomes (Katsinas, Tollefson, & Reamey, 2008).

Student-Centered Approaches

There will be a continued shift towards student-centered approaches that prioritize the needs and experiences of students. This shift involves the implementation of personalized learning plans, which tailor educational experiences to individual student goals, learning styles, and paces. Personalized learning can include adaptive learning technologies, competency-based education, and individualized academic advising that helps students create and follow a customized academic path. By focusing on the unique needs of each student, community colleges can enhance engagement, improve retention rates, and support diverse learning preferences.

Flexible scheduling is another critical component of this student-centered approach. Offering classes during evenings, weekends, and online allows students to balance their studies with work, family responsibilities, and other commitments. This flexibility is particularly important for non-traditional students, such as working adults and parents, who require adaptable options to pursue their education. Additionally, comprehensive support services that address both academic and non-academic needs are essential. These services can include tutoring, career counseling, mental health resources, childcare, and financial aid assistance. By providing holistic support, community colleges can help students overcome barriers to their education, ensuring they have the resources needed to succeed.

Community colleges will focus on creating inclusive, supportive environments that foster student success. This involves building a campus culture that values diversity, equity, and inclusion, ensuring that all students feel welcome and respected. Initiatives such as diversity training for faculty and staff, student resource centers, and inclusive curriculum development are crucial. Moreover, fostering strong relationships between students and faculty through mentorship programs and active learning opportunities can create a sense of belonging and community. By adopting these student-centered approaches, community colleges can create an environment where every student can thrive, ultimately leading to higher graduation rates and better long-term outcomes (Kuh, Kinzie, Schuh, & Whitt, 2010).

Potential Areas for Innovation

Community colleges are continuously seeking innovative approaches to improve student success and meet workforce needs. Potential areas for innovation include:

Competency-Based Education (CBE)

CBE programs allow students to progress at their own pace by demonstrating mastery of specific skills and knowledge. This approach can benefit adult learners and those with prior work experience, providing a more flexible and personalized learning pathway (Johnstone & Soares, 2014).

Technology-Enhanced Learning

Leveraging advanced technologies such as artificial intelligence, virtual reality, and augmented reality can significantly enhance the learning experience. These technologies create immersive learning environments, provide real-time feedback, and support adaptive learning platforms tailored to individual student needs (Means, Bakia, & Murphy, 2014).

Integrated Student Support Services

Developing holistic support systems that integrate academic advising, career counseling, mental health services, and financial aid can help address the diverse needs of community college students. Innovative models like the "one-stop shop" approach can streamline access to these services and improve overall student outcomes (Karp, 2011).

Work-Based Learning

Expanding opportunities for work-based learning, such as internships, apprenticeships, and cooperative education programs, is essential for enhancing student employability by providing practical, hands-on experience. These programs allow students to apply theoretical knowledge in real-world settings, develop relevant skills, and build professional networks. Partnerships with local businesses and industries are crucial for aligning these opportunities with labor market demands, ensuring that students acquire the skills and knowledge needed by employers. These collaborations benefit both students and employers, creating a pipeline of well-prepared, motivated potential employees and fostering economic growth and community development (Soares, 2013).

Open Educational Resources (OER)

Adopting Open Educational Resources (OER) can significantly reduce the cost of textbooks and other course materials, making education more affordable and accessible for students. The high cost of traditional textbooks often poses a financial barrier for students, leading to situations where they may forgo purchasing required materials, thereby negatively impacting their academic performance. By utilizing OER, which are freely available and openly licensed educational materials, institutions can alleviate this burden, allowing students to access necessary resources without additional financial strain.

Moreover, OER provides faculty with the flexibility to customize and update course materials to better align with their specific teaching objectives and the needs of their students. Unlike traditional textbooks, which may quickly become outdated, OER can be continuously revised and improved, incorporating the latest research, industry developments, and pedagogical advancements. This adaptability ensures that course content remains relevant and engaging, enhancing the overall learning experience.

The use of OER also promotes a more inclusive and equitable learning environment. Since OER can be accessed by anyone, they level the playing field, giving all students, regardless of their economic background, the opportunity to succeed. Faculty can tailor OER to address diverse learning styles and cultural perspectives, making the educational content more relatable and effective for a wider range of students.

Furthermore, the collaborative nature of OER encourages academic sharing and innovation. Faculty members can contribute to and benefit from a global community of educators, sharing best practices and resources. This collective effort not only enriches the quality of the educational materials but also fosters a culture of continuous improvement and professional development among educators.

In summary, adopting OER can make education more affordable by reducing the cost of textbooks and other course materials. It empowers faculty to customize and update content to better meet the needs of their courses and students, promotes inclusivity and equity in education, and encourages academic collaboration and innovation. As such, the integration of OER is a vital step toward creating a more accessible, relevant, and dynamic educational landscape (Hilton, 2016).

Reforms Needed to Meet Future Demands

Community colleges must implement several key reforms to meet future education and workforce demands. These reforms include curriculum modernization, which involves updating and aligning curricula with current industry standards and emerging technologies, as well as introducing courses in high-demand fields such as cybersecurity, renewable energy, healthcare, and advanced manufacturing. Building strong partnerships with local businesses and industries is essential to ensure training programs meet actual workforce needs, facilitating internships, apprenticeships, and job placement opportunities for students.

Enhanced career services are also crucial, providing robust career counseling and job placement services to help students transition smoothly from education to employment. This includes offering career workshops, resume writing assistance, and interview preparation.

Flexible learning options, such as online, hybrid, and evening classes, should be made available to accommodate the diverse schedules of students, along with implementing stackable credentials that allow students to earn certificates and degrees in stages.

Focusing on the development of soft skills like communication, teamwork, and problem-solving is essential, with partnerships with employers to identify the most in-demand soft skills. Ensuring access and equity in educational opportunities for all students, including underserved and marginalized communities, is vital. This involves providing support services such as tutoring, mentorship, and financial aid to help all students succeed.

Investing in state-of-the-art technology and infrastructure to support modern teaching methods and learning environments is necessary, along with encouraging faculty to adopt and integrate innovative teaching tools and techniques. Offering continuous professional development opportunities for faculty to keep them updated on the latest industry trends and teaching methodologies, as well as encouraging research and collaboration with industry experts, is key.

Utilizing data analytics to track student outcomes and program effectiveness allows for informed decisions and continuous improvement. Regularly assessing and updating programs based on feedback from students, employers, and community stakeholders ensures the relevance and quality of education. Lastly, engaging with the local community to understand their needs and how the community college can contribute to local economic development, while promoting programs through outreach and public relations efforts, will attract a diverse student population. Implementing these reforms will help community colleges adapt to the evolving educational landscape and better prepare students for the workforce of the future.

Reforming Funding Models

Advocating for increased public funding, exploring alternative funding sources, and implementing performance-based funding models that reward institutions for improving student outcomes are essential strategies for ensuring the financial sustainability and effectiveness of educational institutions. Increased public funding is crucial for maintaining and enhancing the quality of education, supporting infrastructure development, and ensuring that institutions can provide necessary resources and services to students. This funding can help reduce the financial burden on students and their families, making higher education more accessible and equitable.

Exploring alternative funding sources is another vital approach. Educational institutions can diversify their revenue streams by seeking grants from private foundations, engaging in public-private partnerships, and launching fundraising campaigns. Additionally, institutions can generate income through auxiliary enterprises such as campus housing, dining services, and continuing education programs. These alternative sources of funding can provide financial stability and reduce reliance on fluctuating public funding levels.

Implementing performance-based funding models is an innovative strategy that aligns financial incentives with institutional goals of improving student outcomes. These models allocate funds based on specific performance metrics, such as graduation rates, job placement rates, and student retention. By linking funding to measurable outcomes, institutions are motivated to adopt best practices, enhance student support services, and focus on strategies that lead to student success. Performance-based funding encourages accountability and ensures that public investments in education yield tangible results.

In summary, advocating for increased public funding, exploring alternative funding sources, and implementing performance-based funding models are essential strategies for supporting the financial health and effectiveness of educational institutions. These approaches not only ensure that institutions have the necessary resources to provide high-quality education but also promote accountability and continuous improvement in student outcomes (Dougherty & Reddy, 2013).

Developing Clear Degree Pathways

Creating guided pathways that map out the courses and experiences needed to achieve specific credentials or degrees can significantly help students navigate their educational journey more effectively, thereby reducing excess credits and shortening the time to completion. Guided pathways provide a clear, structured roadmap of the academic and career steps students need to take; from the moment they enroll until they achieve their educational goals. These pathways outline the specific courses, sequence, and critical milestones necessary for students to complete their programs efficiently.

By clearly defining the academic requirements and timelines, guided pathways help students make informed decisions about their course selections and educational plans. This structured approach minimizes the likelihood of students taking unnecessary or redundant courses, which can lead to wasted time and increased educational costs. Additionally, guided pathways can help prevent students from feeling overwhelmed or lost in their educational pursuits, offering a more streamlined and supportive experience.

Guided pathways also integrate academic advising and support services, ensuring that students receive consistent guidance throughout their educational journey. Advisors play a crucial role in helping students understand their pathway, monitor their progress, and make adjustments as needed. This proactive advising model helps identify and address potential obstacles early, reducing the risk of students dropping out or delaying their completion.

Furthermore, guided pathways can include opportunities for experiential learning, such as internships, co-ops, and service-learning projects, which are aligned with students' academic and career goals. These experiences provide practical, hands-on learning opportunities that enhance students' skills and employability while ensuring that their educational journey is relevant and engaging.

By implementing guided pathways, educational institutions can improve student retention and graduation rates. Clear pathways help students stay focused and motivated, as they can see a direct connection between their coursework and their career aspirations. This approach also promotes equity, as it provides all students, regardless of their background or prior knowledge, with a clear and accessible route to success.

In summary, creating guided pathways that map out the courses and experiences needed to achieve specific credentials or degrees can significantly enhance students' ability to navigate their educational journey effectively. By reducing excess credits and time to completion, guided pathways provide a structured, supportive, and efficient route to achieving educational goals, ultimately improving student outcomes and success (Bailey, Jaggars, & Jenkins, 2015).

Utilizing Data Analytics

Investing in robust data systems and training staff to use data effectively is crucial for community colleges to identify trends, assess program effectiveness, and implement targeted interventions. Advanced data systems enable institutions to collect, store, and analyze vast amounts of information related to student performance, enrollment patterns, and educational outcomes. This data-driven approach provides invaluable insights that can inform decision-making and strategic planning.

By investing in state-of-the-art data systems, community colleges can track and monitor various aspects of their operations in real-time. For instance, data on student demographics, course enrollments, completion rates, and post-graduation employment can be systematically collected and analyzed. This comprehensive data collection allows colleges to identify emerging trends and patterns, such as shifts in student populations, changes in enrollment numbers, or areas where students may be struggling academically.

Training staff to effectively use these data systems is equally important. Staff must be proficient in data analytics to interpret the information accurately and make informed decisions. This training ensures that faculty and administrative staff can leverage data to enhance their programs and services. For example, academic advisors can use data to identify students at risk of dropping out and intervene with targeted support, such as tutoring or counseling. Instructors can use data to refine their teaching methods and curricula, ensuring that they meet the needs of their students.

Data analytics play a pivotal role in assessing program effectiveness. By analyzing data on student outcomes, community colleges can evaluate the success of their academic programs and support services. This evaluation helps identify which programs are performing well and which ones need improvement. For instance, if data reveals that a particular course has a high failure rate, the institution can investigate the underlying causes and implement changes to improve student success, such as revising the curriculum or providing additional resources.

Furthermore, data-driven decision-making supports the implementation of targeted interventions. Community colleges can use data to design and execute initiatives aimed at addressing specific challenges. For example, if data indicates that certain student groups, such as first-generation college students or minority students, are underperforming, the college can develop tailored support programs to help these students succeed. These interventions might include mentorship programs, financial aid workshops, or specialized academic support services.

Overall, investing in robust data systems and training staff to use data effectively is essential for continuous improvement in community colleges. This approach enables institutions to make evidence-based decisions, optimize their resources, and enhance the quality of education and support they provide. By leveraging data analytics, community colleges can better serve their students, improve outcomes, and fulfill their mission of providing accessible and high-quality education (McKay & Devlin, 2016).

Promoting Equity and Inclusion

Implementing policies and practices that promote equity and inclusion is essential for ensuring all students have the opportunity to succeed. This process begins with recognizing and addressing systemic barriers that disproportionately affect certain student groups. Socioeconomic disparities can significantly hinder students' ability to afford tuition, textbooks, and other educational expenses, thereby limiting their access to higher education. To combat this, community colleges can implement policies such as need-based scholarships, affordable tuition plans, and emergency financial aid programs. These initiatives help alleviate the financial burdens that often prevent low-income students from enrolling and persisting in their studies.

Addressing racial inequalities is another critical aspect of promoting equity and inclusion. This involves creating an institutional culture that actively works against racism and discrimination. Community colleges can implement diversity training for faculty and staff, ensuring that they are equipped to support students from diverse racial and ethnic backgrounds. Additionally, colleges can establish programs and services specifically designed to support underrepresented and marginalized student populations. This includes initiatives such as mentoring programs for students of color, culturally responsive counseling services, and student organizations that provide a sense of community and belonging.

Providing targeted support for underrepresented and marginalized students is also crucial. These supports can take many forms, including academic assistance through tutoring and supplemental instruction, as well as non-academic support such as mental health services, childcare, and transportation assistance. By addressing the unique challenges faced by these students, community colleges can create a more inclusive environment that supports their academic and personal success.

Furthermore, data-driven approaches can help identify gaps in equity and inclusion efforts. Regularly collecting and analyzing data on student outcomes by race, gender, socioeconomic status, and other factors allows institutions to pinpoint where disparities exist and measure the effectiveness of their interventions. This ongoing assessment ensures that policies and practices are continually refined to better serve all students.

In conclusion, promoting equity and inclusion requires a multifaceted approach that addresses both systemic barriers and the specific needs of underrepresented and marginalized students. By implementing comprehensive policies and practices, community colleges can create an educational environment where all students have the opportunity to succeed, leading to more equitable outcomes across the board (Bensimon, 2005).

Investing in Professional Development

Implementing policies and practices that promote equity and inclusion is essential for ensuring all students have the opportunity to succeed. This process begins with recognizing and addressing systemic barriers that disproportionately affect certain student groups. Socioeconomic disparities can significantly hinder students' ability to afford tuition, textbooks, and other educational expenses, thereby limiting their access to higher education. To combat this, community colleges can implement policies such as need-based scholarships, affordable tuition plans, and emergency financial aid programs. These initiatives help alleviate the financial burdens that often prevent low-income students from enrolling and persisting in their studies.

Addressing racial inequalities is another critical aspect of promoting equity and inclusion. This involves creating an institutional culture that actively works against racism and discrimination. Community colleges can implement diversity training for faculty and staff, ensuring that they are equipped to support students from diverse racial and ethnic backgrounds. Additionally, colleges can establish programs and services specifically designed to support underrepresented and marginalized student populations. This includes initiatives such as mentoring programs for students of color, culturally responsive counseling services, and student organizations that provide a sense of community and belonging.

Providing targeted support for underrepresented and marginalized students is also crucial. These supports can take many forms, including academic assistance through tutoring and supplemental instruction, as well as non-academic support such as mental health services, childcare, and transportation assistance. By addressing the unique challenges faced by these students, community colleges can create a more inclusive environment that supports their academic and personal success. Furthermore, data-driven approaches can help identify gaps in equity and inclusion efforts. Regularly collecting and analyzing data on student outcomes by race, gender, socioeconomic status, and other factors allows institutions to pinpoint where disparities exist and measure the effectiveness of their interventions. This ongoing assessment ensures that policies and practices are continually refined to better serve all students.

In addition to these measures, professional development for community college faculty is crucial for fostering innovation and improving teaching and learning practices. Ongoing training in new pedagogical approaches ensures that faculty can adapt to evolving educational landscapes and meet the diverse needs of their students. This includes training in active learning strategies, culturally responsive teaching, and inclusive pedagogies that engage all learners. Technology integration is another critical area of professional development. Faculty must be adept at using digital tools and online platforms to enhance the learning experience, especially in an increasingly digital world. This includes training in using learning management systems, virtual collaboration tools, and multimedia resources effectively.

Professional development also focuses on strategies for supporting diverse learners. Faculty need to understand the unique challenges faced by students from various backgrounds and be equipped with the tools to support them effectively. This can include training on implicit bias, strategies for creating inclusive classroom environments, and methods for providing differentiated instruction. By investing in professional development, community colleges can ensure that their faculty are well-prepared to meet the needs of all students, fostering a more inclusive and supportive educational environment.

In conclusion, promoting equity and inclusion requires a multifaceted approach that addresses both systemic barriers and the specific needs of underrepresented and marginalized students. By implementing comprehensive policies and practices, along with robust professional development for faculty, community colleges can create an educational environment where all students have the opportunity to succeed, leading to more equitable outcomes across the board (Bensimon, 2005; Cox, McIntosh, Terenzini, Reason, & Quaye, 2010).

Comparison with International Models

Community colleges in the United States can benefit from comparing their educational models with those of other countries to identify areas for improvement and innovation. For instance, Germany's dual education system effectively integrates vocational training and academic education, resulting in a highly skilled workforce (Euler, 2013). In this system, students split their time between classroom instruction and hands-on training with an employer, ensuring that they gain both theoretical knowledge and practical skills. This dual approach not only enhances the employability of graduates but also aligns educational outcomes with the specific needs of the labor market, fostering a direct pathway from education to employment.

Similarly, Australia's Technical and Further Education (TAFE) system provides a model for aligning vocational courses with labor market needs through extensive industry collaboration (Smith, 2010). TAFE institutions work closely with employers to design courses that meet current industry standards and expectations, ensuring that graduates are well-prepared for the workforce. This close cooperation with industry partners helps to keep curricula up-to-date and relevant, providing students with the skills and knowledge that are in demand. Moreover, TAFE institutions often offer flexible learning options, including part-time and online courses, making vocational education accessible to a wider range of students, including those who are already employed or have other commitments.

By studying these international models, U.S. community colleges can explore ways to enhance their vocational training programs, improve industry partnerships, and create more robust pathways from education to employment. For example, adopting elements of Germany's dual education system could involve developing more structured apprenticeship programs that combine classroom learning with on-the-job training. This would provide students with real-world experience and a smoother transition into the workforce. Similarly, by emulating the TAFE system's strong industry collaboration, U.S. community colleges can work more closely with local businesses and industries to ensure that their programs are aligned with market needs, thereby improving job placement rates for graduates.

Additionally, these comparisons can inspire U.S. community colleges to innovate in areas such as curriculum development, teaching methods, and student support services. For instance, integrating industry-recognized certifications and credentials into vocational programs can enhance the value of a community college education and make graduates more attractive to employers. Implementing robust career counseling and job placement services, similar to those in Australia's TAFE system, can also help students navigate their career paths more effectively. By leveraging the strengths of international educational models, U.S. community colleges can develop more comprehensive and effective strategies to meet the evolving demands of the global economy and ensure that their students are well-equipped for success.

Learning from Global Best Practices

Adopting successful strategies and innovations from around the world can improve the effectiveness of U.S. community colleges. Key practices include:

- **Emphasis on Lifelong Learning:** Finland and Singapore focus on adult education and continuous skill development, supporting individuals in updating their skills throughout their careers (Nuissl & Pehl, 2004; Chong, 2016).

- **Use of Educational Technology:** South Korea and Estonia have invested heavily in educational technology, improving educational outcomes and making learning more flexible and accessible (OECD, 2015).

- **Equity and Inclusion:** Canada and the Netherlands have implemented comprehensive support systems to ensure that all students have access to quality education and the resources they need to succeed (Finnie, Usher, & Vossensteyn, 2014). By adopting these best practices, U.S. community colleges can enhance their efforts to promote equity and inclusion, ensuring that all students can achieve their educational and career goals.

Failure is not an option when it comes to the education of the masses—after all, who wants a world full of professional couch potatoes? Community colleges must offer a streamlined and supportive experience through guided pathways, integrating academic advising and support services to keep students from feeling like they've wandered into an academic labyrinth. Proactive advising is like having a GPS for your education, helping address potential obstacles early and reducing dropout risks and delays. Experiential learning opportunities aligned with academic and career goals enhance students' skills and employability, because who wouldn't want to graduate with more than just the ability to ace Netflix marathons?

Robust data systems and staff training in data analytics are crucial for identifying trends, assessing program effectiveness, and implementing targeted interventions. Think of it as turning community colleges into educational versions of Sherlock Holmes, but with less pipe smoking. This data-driven approach supports evidence-based decision-making and continuous improvement, because guessing just isn't as effective. Promoting equity and inclusion by addressing systemic barriers and providing targeted support for underrepresented students is essential—no one should feel like they're playing educational dodgeball without a team. Ongoing training in new pedagogical approaches and technology integration fosters innovation, transforming classrooms from chalkboards to hoverboards (okay, maybe not hoverboards, but you get the idea).

Chapter 9

Cornerstones of Opportunity: Critical Role in Higher Education

Community colleges are the unsung heroes of the American higher education landscape, offering accessible and affordable educational opportunities to a diverse student population. Their superpower? Lower tuition costs compared to four-year universities, making higher education more attainable for everyone from high school grads to retired rockstars looking to finally get that degree in astrophysics. Financial aid options, like scholarships and grants, add extra magic, reducing the financial burden on students and making education feel less like a financial black hole. By promoting educational equity and social mobility, community colleges are basically the educational version of a superhero squad, fighting for the academic dreams of the everyday citizen.

These institutions serve a varied student body, including recent high school graduates, adult learners, working professionals, and individuals seeking career changes. Community colleges are known for their inclusivity, providing targeted support for minority, low-income, and first-generation college students. They offer flexible class schedules, including evening, weekend, and online classes, catering to non-traditional students. This flexibility allows students to balance their studies with personal and professional commitments, choosing between part-time and full-time enrollment as needed.

Community colleges are vital for workforce development, offering vocational and technical training programs that provide practical skills and training for various industries, such as healthcare, technology, and manufacturing. Collaboration with local businesses and industries ensures that these programs align with current job market needs, enhancing students' employability. Additionally, many community colleges have transfer agreements with four-year universities, facilitating the transfer process and ensuring that credits earned are transferable. Dual enrollment programs allow high school students to take community college courses and earn college credits, accelerating their educational journey.

These institutions are deeply embedded in their local communities, offering programs and services that meet the specific needs of the area. They provide continuing education and lifelong learning opportunities, including adult education, professional development, and personal enrichment courses. Comprehensive student support services, such as academic advising, tutoring, career counseling, and mental health services, are commonly available to support student success. Some colleges offer integrated support services in a single location, streamlining access and improving student outcomes.

Community colleges are also known for their innovation and adaptability, increasingly adopting educational technologies, such as online learning platforms, to enhance teaching and learning. Their programs are regularly updated to reflect industry changes, ensuring that students acquire relevant and up-to-date skills. They play a vital role in local economic development by providing job training and placement services that meet the needs of regional employers and help address workforce shortages in critical areas like healthcare, IT, and skilled trades through targeted training programs.

The Continuing Importance of Community Colleges

Community colleges remain a cornerstone of the higher education system, playing a vital role in providing accessible, affordable, and high-quality education to a diverse student population. Their continuing importance is underscored by several key factors:

Accessibility and Affordability

Community colleges offer an affordable alternative to four-year universities, making higher education accessible to a broader range of students, including those from low-income backgrounds. The lower tuition costs and availability of financial aid make it possible for many students to pursue postsecondary education without incurring substantial debt. This affordability is crucial in promoting educational equity and social mobility, as it opens doors for individuals who might otherwise be unable to afford higher education.

Flexibility and Support for Non-Traditional Students

Community colleges are known for their flexible scheduling options, including evening, weekend, and online classes, which cater to non-traditional students such as working adults, parents, and those returning to education after a break. This flexibility allows students to balance their studies with work and family responsibilities. Additionally, community colleges often provide extensive support services, including tutoring, academic advising, and career counseling, to help students succeed.

Workforce Development and Vocational Training

Community colleges play a pivotal role in workforce development by offering vocational training and certificate programs that are closely aligned with local labor market needs. These programs equip students with practical skills and credentials that enhance their employability and meet the demands of various industries. By partnering with local businesses and industries, community colleges ensure that their curricula remain relevant and responsive to economic trends, thereby supporting local economies and filling critical workforce gaps.

Pathways to Higher Education

Community colleges serve as important steppingstones for students aspiring to earn a bachelor's degree. Many students begin their postsecondary education at a community college and then transfer to a four-year institution to complete their degree. Articulation agreements between community colleges and universities facilitate smooth transitions and ensure that credits earned are transferable. This pathway is particularly beneficial for students who may not be ready or able to attend a four-year institution immediately after high school.

Community Engagement and Lifelong Learning

Community colleges are deeply embedded in their local communities, providing not only educational opportunities but also cultural, recreational, and social services. They often host community events, offer continuing education and adult learning programs, and serve as hubs for community engagement. This commitment to lifelong learning and community service helps to foster a more educated and engaged citizenry.

Addressing Workforce Shortages

In areas facing critical workforce shortages, such as healthcare, information technology, and advanced manufacturing, community colleges are instrumental in training and certifying professionals to fill these gaps. By offering specialized programs and fast-track training options, they help to quickly address workforce needs and support economic development.

In summary, community colleges are essential to the higher education system, providing accessible, affordable, and flexible educational opportunities that promote social mobility, support workforce development, and serve as gateways to further education. Their ongoing contributions are vital to the educational and economic well-being of communities across the nation.

Final Thoughts and Call to Action for American Community Colleges

American community colleges are indispensable in the higher education landscape, providing accessible, affordable, and flexible education to a diverse range of students. Their role in promoting social mobility, supporting workforce development, and fostering lifelong learning is unparalleled. As the educational and economic demands of society continue to evolve, community colleges must adapt and innovate to meet these challenges head-on.

Community colleges are uniquely positioned to address some of the most pressing issues in higher education and the workforce. They offer a crucial pathway for students from all backgrounds to achieve their educational and career goals. By providing affordable education, tailored support services, and programs aligned with labor market needs, community colleges play a vital role in ensuring that higher education remains inclusive and relevant. Their commitment to equity and access helps to bridge the gap between underrepresented and marginalized populations, fostering a more educated and equitable society.

To sustain and enhance the impact of community colleges, stakeholders must prioritize several key actions:

- **Increased Funding:** Federal, state, and local governments must recognize the importance of community colleges and allocate sufficient funding to support their operations and growth. This includes investing in infrastructure, technology, and student support services to ensure that these institutions can provide high-quality education and meet the needs of their students.

- **Strengthen Partnerships:** Community colleges should continue to build and strengthen partnerships with local businesses and industries. These collaborations are essential for aligning educational programs with workforce demands, providing students with practical experience, and enhancing their employability.

- **Promote Equity and Inclusion:** Efforts to promote equity and inclusion must be intensified. This includes implementing policies and practices that support underrepresented students, addressing barriers to education, and ensuring that all students have access to the resources they need to succeed.

- **Embrace Innovation:** Embracing innovative educational models and technologies that enhance learning and accessibility is crucial. Community colleges should explore competency-based education, blended learning, and other flexible delivery methods that cater to the diverse needs of their students.

- **Engage in Advocacy:** Engaging in advocacy efforts to influence public policy and secure the support needed for community colleges to thrive is essential. This includes lobbying for increased funding, favorable legislation, and policies that recognize the critical role of community colleges in higher education and workforce development. By taking these steps, community colleges can continue to fulfill their mission and expand their impact, helping to create a more educated, skilled, and equitable society. The future of community colleges is bright, but it requires collective action and commitment from all stakeholders to realize their full potential.

American community colleges cannot fail in the education of the masses—because who else is going to save us from a future where everyone has a PhD in YouTube tutorials? They remain the backbone of the American higher education system, providing accessible, affordable, and flexible education to a diverse student population. Think of them as the Swiss Army knife of education: promoting social mobility, supporting workforce development, and serving as gateways to further education.

Their superpower? Making higher education affordable! With financial aid options like scholarships and grants, they help students avoid the dreaded student debt black hole. Plus, their flexible scheduling and extensive support services cater to non-traditional students, allowing them to juggle personal and professional commitments without turning into stressed-out zombies. Guided pathways integrate academic advising and support services to keep students from feeling like they've wandered into an educational maze with no exit.

Robust data systems and staff training in data analytics? Oh yes, because nothing says "we got this" like a college armed with Sherlock Holmes-level data sleuthing skills. By adopting successful strategies from international models and focusing on lifelong learning, educational technology, and comprehensive support systems, community colleges can continue to be the educational superheroes promoting equity and inclusion. As educational and economic demands evolve, these institutions must adapt and innovate, ensuring they remain a critical resource for students and communities nationwide. Maintaining high academic standards, proper accreditation, and overcoming funding and resource allocation challenges are vital. Ultimately, their success is essential for the future of their students and communities.

And finally, there you have it: community colleges are the heroes of American higher education, valiantly serving up affordable, flexible, and high-quality education like it's their superpower. Meanwhile, four-year universities, perched on their ivory towers, might see community colleges as mere underlings in the academic realm. But let's be real—if community colleges were a superhero team, they'd be the Avengers, while some universities are still trying to figure out their superhero names. It's high time universities stopped fighting these educational superheroes and started embracing them as vital partners in student success. After all, if we're talking about saving the day in education, who needs another high-priced, high-maintenance superhero when you've got community colleges, wielding their mighty low tuition and flexible schedules to rescue students from the clutches of debt and disillusionment? Together, they can form the ultimate academic alliance, ensuring that every student gets the hero's journey they deserve.

Chapter 10

The Path Forward: Overcoming Challenges, Embracing Opportunities

T he evolution of American community colleges reads like an epic saga in the world of higher education. These institutions have heroically fulfilled their mission to provide accessible, affordable, and flexible education to a diverse population, deftly adapting to the ever-changing educational, economic, and social needs of the nation. From their humble beginnings as a bridge between high school and university education to their current status as essential pillars of workforce development and social mobility, community colleges have proven themselves indispensable. They're like the Swiss Army knives of education, offering a wide range of programs tailored to local job markets, helping students gain practical skills and boost their employability.

But wait, there's more! Community colleges also play a critical role in democratizing education by serving non-traditional students—think working adults, first-generation college students, and those from underserved communities. It's like they rolled out the red carpet for everyone who thought higher education was out of reach. So, here's to community colleges, the unsung heroes of the academic world, proving that you don't need an Ivy League name to make a massive impact.

Community colleges face significant challenges. The high failure rate of students, coupled with substantial debt burdens, highlights the need for comprehensive support systems and better financial aid structures. Many students encounter significant barriers, such as balancing work, family responsibilities, and academic commitments, which can impede their progress and lead to high dropout rates. Furthermore, faculty and institutions often struggle with limited resources, inadequate funding, and bureaucratic obstacles that hinder their success and effectiveness. Institutional barriers, such as inconsistent course availability and transfer credit issues, further complicate the educational journey for many students, making it difficult for them to complete their programs on time or transfer credits seamlessly to four-year institutions.

Leadership within these colleges, often shaped by practical Ed.D. programs, plays a crucial role in navigating these challenges and driving the institutions forward. Despite their practical training, leaders holding Ed.D. degrees often lack the innovative leadership and managerial abilities needed to effectively address these issues. This deficiency can lead to power struggles at the top, as leaders compete for positions rather than focusing on institutional improvement and student success. Effective leadership should prioritize fostering a collaborative environment, promoting innovation, and focusing on strategic initiatives that enhance the overall student experience and institutional performance.

As community colleges look to the future, addressing these persistent issues is paramount. Their ongoing commitment to accessibility, equity, and lifelong learning, coupled with strategic improvements in support services, resource allocation, and leadership development, will be essential. Ensuring student success and institutional effectiveness will solidify the role of community colleges as vital contributors to the educational and economic well-being of their communities and the nation. By leveraging technology, expanding partnerships with industry, and continuously evolving to meet the needs of their diverse student populations, community colleges can continue to be a beacon of opportunity and a catalyst for personal and professional growth.

The failure of community colleges is simply not on the table, as their evolution represents a transformative chapter in higher education—like the plot twist everyone loves. These institutions must dodge significant challenges, such as high student failure rates and limited resources, to keep being the superheroes of workforce development and social mobility. By prioritizing student success and institutional effectiveness through strategic improvements in support services, resource allocation, and leadership development, community colleges can continue to serve as vital contributors to the educational and economic well-being of their communities and the nation.

Community colleges are a crucial touchpoint for student success, but they need a major makeover. They should transform from just being transfer hubs into standalone four-year bachelor's degree powerhouses or get hitched directly to universities. This way, students won't lose momentum and can stay on track to their degrees without feeling like they're stuck in academic limbo. Because, let's face it, if community colleges don't succeed, we might as well start preparing for a future where professional Netflix binging is a legitimate career option. And no one wants to see that on a resume, unless you're applying for the role of Chief Couch Potato!

Chapter 11

Embracing the Future: Embracing Community College Evolution

C ommunity colleges have emerged as the unsung heroes of higher education, continually adapting to provide accessible, affordable, and flexible educational opportunities. By offering bachelor's degrees, these institutions are tackling local workforce needs and giving non-traditional students a shot at academic and career success without the usual financial and logistical headaches of traditional four-year schools. Despite wrestling with issues like transferability and funding constraints, community colleges are crucial for serving a diverse crowd, including non-traditional students, first-generation college goers, and those from low-income backgrounds.

Addressing these challenges? Well, that's like trying to solve a Rubik's Cube blindfolded. It requires a multifaceted approach: more financial support from state and federal governments, smoother transfer agreements, comprehensive support services, and some out-of-the-box funding strategies. Focusing on student success, retention, and completion rates through measures like the Guided Pathways model, robust advising services, and leveraging data for decision-making is key. Think of it as turning community colleges into academic superheroes. Emphasizing equity and inclusion, inspired by education systems in countries like Canada and the Netherlands, can further supercharge the mission of community colleges. So, move over to traditional universities—community colleges are here to save the day, one student at a time!

Evolution of Community Colleges: Standalone Institutions vs. University Integration

The debate over whether community colleges should remain standalone institutions or become part of larger university systems includes several significant benefits. Standalone community colleges maintain a distinct identity focused on local needs and a more intimate, community-oriented environment, allowing them to swiftly adapt to changes in local workforce demands and provide personalized support to students. This flexibility helps to foster a sense of community and enables rapid implementation of program changes to meet local economic and job market needs (College Values Online, 2024; U.S. Bureau of Labor Statistics, 2024). Furthermore, standalone status allows these colleges to offer tailored programs and services that directly address the specific needs of their communities, ensuring that students receive relevant and practical education that aligns with local employment opportunities (College Values Online, 2024; Career Center Penn West, 2024).

On the other hand, integrating community colleges into larger university systems can offer several advantages, including increased funding, access to better facilities, and more substantial academic resources, which can enhance educational offerings and institutional stability (Career Center Penn West, 2024; U.S. Bureau of Labor Statistics, 2024). Such integration facilitates seamless credit transfer for students, ensuring that the credits earned at the community college level are fully recognized and applied towards a bachelor's degree, thus providing a smoother academic progression (College Values Online, 2024). Additionally, becoming part of a larger system can open up research opportunities and advanced academic programs that might not be available at standalone community colleges, offering students a more comprehensive educational experience (Career Center Penn West, 2024).

However, this integration must be managed carefully to ensure that the unique mission of community colleges—focusing on accessibility and serving non-traditional students—is not compromised (U.S. Bureau of Labor Statistics, 2024). Administrative challenges during the merging process, along with potential mission drift towards traditional academic goals, could disrupt the core strengths and operations of community colleges (College Values Online, 2024).

As these institutions look to the future, addressing transferability issues is critical for student success. Many students at community colleges aspire to transfer to four-year institutions to continue their education, yet inconsistent credit transfer policies can hinder this progression. Improved articulation agreements between community colleges and universities are essential to ensure seamless transitions for students, maximizing their chances of academic and career success.

Moreover, comprehensive support services play a pivotal role in student success. Robust advising services, tutoring, career counseling, and mental health resources can significantly impact retention and completion rates. By creating an environment that supports students holistically, community colleges can help students overcome personal and academic challenges, leading to higher success rates.

The collective action and commitment of all stakeholders are paramount to realizing the full potential of community colleges in creating a more educated, skilled, equitable society, and solid leadership rather than personal career goals. By focusing on accessibility, equity, and lifelong learning, and addressing critical issues such as transferability and comprehensive support, community colleges will continue to be essential contributors to the educational and economic well-being of their communities and the nation.

The debate over whether community colleges should remain standalone institutions or integrate into larger university systems involves weighing significant benefits on both sides. Standalone community colleges excel in maintaining a distinct identity focused on local needs, providing a community-oriented environment that adapts swiftly to local workforce demands. This flexibility fosters a sense of community and allows for rapid program changes to meet local economic needs. On the other hand, integrating into larger university systems offers increased funding, better facilities, and more substantial academic resources, which can enhance educational offerings and institutional stability. Community colleges are at the forefront of a transformative era in higher education, tasked with the mission of providing accessible, affordable, and flexible education to a diverse population through:

- **No Room for Failure:** Community colleges cannot afford to fail, given their pivotal role in higher education.
- **Transformative Evolution:** They represent a transformative chapter in fulfilling the mission of accessible, affordable, and flexible education for a diverse population.
- **Challenges to Overcome:** Significant challenges include high student failure rates and limited resources.

- **Pillars of Workforce Development:** Essential for workforce development and social mobility.
- **Prioritizing Success:** Focus on student success and institutional effectiveness through improvements in support services, resource allocation, and leadership development.
- **Vital Contributors:** Essential to the educational and economic well-being of communities and the nation.

Ultimately, strong leadership is essential for community colleges to navigate their evolving role in higher education and to preserve their unique mission of accessibility and practical education. This might mean forming closer ties with larger university systems—because, hey, who doesn't love a little more red tape? The current model, with its outdated practices, is a recipe for failure. Community colleges either need a major upgrade to become standalone four-year bachelorette institutions only or should be bolted directly onto universities. This will ensure that students don't lose momentum and can smoothly progress toward their degrees.

If the aim is to keep the community college mission unchanged for nostalgic reasons—even at the expense of student success—then shame on them but, a major overhaul is needed to prevent community colleges from becoming obsolete. At the end of the day, student success must take priority over personal career goals, power plays, and institutional turf wars. After all, who wouldn't want an education system that can juggle flaming torches while riding a unicycle? It sounds like the perfect setup for a smooth educational journey, right?

"There are no secrets to success. It is the result of preparation, hard work, and learning from failure." ~Colin Powell

Bibliography

Adams, M. (2018). *Employee morale and motivation in educational institutions.* Educational Leadership Review, 45(2), 112-125.

AdLit. (n.d.). *Academic rigor: At the heart of college access and success.* Retrieved from https://www.adlit.org/topics/college-and-career-readiness/academic-rigor

Allen, I. E., & Seaman, J. (2013). "Changing Course: Ten Years of Tracking Online Education in the United States." Babson Survey Research Group.

American Association of Community Colleges. (2021). *Community College FAQs.* Retrieved from aacc.nche.edu.

Anderson, R. (2015). *Family Ties in Business: Navigating Personal and Professional Relationships.* Business Horizons.

Arendale, D. (2004). "Mainstreamed Academic Assistance and Enrichment for All Students: The Historical Origins of Learning Assistance Centers." Research for Educational Reform, 9(4), 3-21.

Astin, A. W. (1993). What Matters in College? Four Critical Years Revisited. San Francisco: Jossey-Bass.

Baker, G. A. (2002). Leadership and Administration in Community Colleges. *Community College Review.*

Bailey, T. R., Jenkins, D., & Leinbach, T. (2005). *What We Know About Community College Low-Income and Minority Student Outcomes: Descriptive Statistics from National Surveys.* Community College Research Center.

Bailey, T., Jeong, D. W., & Cho, S.-W. (2010). Referral, enrollment, and completion in developmental education sequences in community colleges. *Economics of Education Review, 29*(2), 255-270.

Bailey, T. R., Jaggars, S. S., & Jenkins, D. (2015). *Redesigning America's Community Colleges: A Clearer Path to Student Success.* Harvard University Press.

Barshay, J. (2020). Why so few students transferring from community college to university. The Hechinger Report. Retrieved from https://hechingerreport.org/why-so-few-students-transferring-from-community-college-to-university/

Beach, J. M. (2011). *Gateway to Opportunity? A History of the Community College in the United States.* Stylus Publishing, LLC.

Bensimon, E. M. (2005). "Closing the Achievement Gap in Higher Education: An Organizational Learning Perspective." New Directions for Higher Education, 2005(131), 99-111.

Bettinger, E., & Loeb, S. (2017). Promises and pitfalls of online education. *Brookings Papers on Economic Activity*, 2017(2), 111-168. https://doi.org/10.1353/pea.2017.0014

Boyer, E. L. (1990). *Scholarship reconsidered: Priorities of the professoriate.* The Carnegie Foundation for the Advancement of Teaching.

Bragg, D. D., & Durham, B. (2012). Perspectives on Access and Equity in the Era of (Community) College Completion. *Community College Review*, 40(2), 106-125. Retrieved from SAGE Journals

Brint, S., & Karabel, J. (1989). *The Diverted Dream: Community Colleges and the Promise of Educational Opportunity in America, 1900-1985.* Oxford University Press.

Brown, T. (2019). *Leadership Skills in Higher Education.* Journal of Educational Leadership.

Brown, T. (2020). *Uncertainty in higher education during the pandemic.* Journal of Educational Studies, 35(4), 563-578.

Brown, T., & White, S. (2021). *The Hidden Costs of Nepotism in Leadership.* Journal of Organizational Behavior.

Career Center Penn West. (2024). *Average salary by education level: The value of a college degree.* Retrieved from Career Center Penn West

Carnevale, A. P., Smith, N., & Strohl, J. (2013). Recovery: Job Growth and Education Requirements Through 2020. Georgetown University Center on Education and the Workforce.

Center on Budget and Policy Priorities. (2019, October). *State higher education funding cuts have pushed costs to students, worsened inequality.* Retrieved from https://www.cbpp.org/research/state-budget-and-tax/state-higher-education-funding-cuts-have-pushed-costs-to-students

Chong, E. (2016). "SkillsFuture: Reinvigorating Lifelong Learning in Singapore." Adult Education and Development, 83, 69-72.

Cohen, A. M., Brawer, F. B., & Kisker, C. B. (2013). *The American community college* (6th ed.). Jossey-Bass.

Cohen, A. M., Brawer, F. B., & Kisker, C. B. (2014). *The American Community College.* John Wiley & Sons.

Collaborative Universities. (2024). Exploring leadership practices through case inquiry. *Multiple Universities.* Accessed July 18, 2024. Retrieved from https://example.com

College Board. (n.d.). *Types of scholarships.* Retrieved from https://bigfuture.collegeboard.org/pay-for-college/grants-scholarships/types-of-scholarships

College Board. (2023). Trends in College Pricing and Student Aid 2022. Retrieved from https://research.collegeboard.org/trends/college-pricing

College Values Online. (2024). *Is an associate's degree worth it?* Retrieved from College Values Online

Community College Research Center (CCRC) at Teachers College, Columbia University. (2015). What We Know About Transfer. Retrieved from https://ccrc.tc.columbia.edu/publications/what-we-know-about-transfer.html

Community College Review. (2023). Obtaining your bachelor's degree at a community college. *Community College Review.* Retrieved from [URL]

Connecticut Mirror. (2023). Community colleges in CT are being dismantled. Retrieved from https://ctmirror.org/category/ct-viewpoints/community-colleges-ct-are-being-dismantled

Consumer Financial Protection Bureau. (n.d.). *Private student loans.* Retrieved from https://www.consumerfinance.gov/ask-cfpb/what-is-a-private-student-loan-en-400/

Cox, B. E., McIntosh, K. L., Terenzini, P. T., Reason, R. D., & Quaye, S. J. (2010). "Pedagogical Signals of Faculty Approachability: Factors Shaping Faculty–Student Interaction Outside the Classroom." Research in Higher Education, 51(8), 767-788.

Curtis, M. A. (1960). The Development of Junior Colleges in California. *California State University Press.*

Crosby, E. W. (1930). The Role of Junior Colleges in American Education. *Educational Theory Journal.*

Davis, K. (2021). *Managing Change in Higher Education Institutions.* Educational Management Review.

Davis, K. (2021). *Mental health and student retention in the COVID-19 era.* Journal of Community College Research, 42(3), 245-261.

Davis, R. (2017). *Promoting fairness and equity in community colleges.* Journal of Community College Research, 32(1), 78-89.

Delta Cost Project. (2016, January). *Trends in college spending 2003-2013.* Retrieved from http://www.deltacostproject.org/

Donadel, A. (2023). Why are 87% of these community college students not earning a bachelor's degree? University Business. Retrieved from https://universitybusiness.com/why-are-87-of-these-community-college-students-not-earning-a-bachelors-degree/

Dougherty, K. J., & Townsend, B. K. (2006). Community college missions: A theoretical and historical perspective. *New Directions for Community Colleges, 2006*(136), 5-13.

Dougherty, K. J., & Reddy, V. (2013). "Performance Funding for Higher Education: What Are the Mechanisms? What Are the Impacts?" ASHE Higher Education Report, 39(2), 1-134.

Eddy, P. L., & VanDerLinden, K. E. (2006). *Emerging Definitions of Leadership in Higher Education: New Visions of Leadership or Same Old "Hero" Leader?*. Community College Review, 34(1), 5-26.

Education, NC. (2023). Differences in postsecondary governance models. Retrieved from https://www.ednc.org/differences-in-postsecondary-governance-models

ERIC. (2024). Toxic leadership in educational organizations. *ERIC*. Accessed July 18, 2024. Retrieved from https://eric.ed.gov

Euler, D. (2013). "Germany's Dual Vocational Training System: A Model for Other Countries?" Bertelsmann Stiftung.

Federal Reserve. (2021, December). *Consumer credit – G.19*. Retrieved from https://www.federalreserve.gov/releases/g19/current/

Federal Student Aid. (n.d.-a). *Federal Pell Grants*. Retrieved from https://studentaid.gov/understand-aid/types/grants/pell

Federal Student Aid. (n.d.-b). *Types of federal grants*. Retrieved from https://studentaid.gov/understand-aid/types/grants

Federal Student Aid. (n.d.-c). *Federal work-study jobs*. Retrieved from https://studentaid.gov/understand-aid/types/work-study

Federal Student Aid. (n.d.-d). *Loans*. Retrieved from https://studentaid.gov/understand-aid/types/loans

Finnie, R., Usher, A., & Vossensteyn, H. (2014). "Meeting the Needs of All Students: Inclusive Education in Canada and the Netherlands." Higher Education Management and Policy, 26(2), 1-18.

Gandara, P., Alvarado, E., Driscoll, A., & Orfield, G. (2012). Building pathways to transfer: Community colleges that break the chain of failure for students of color. *The Civil Rights Project at UCLA*.

Garrison, D. R., & Kanuka, H. (2004). "Blended Learning: Uncovering Its Transformative Potential in Higher Education." The Internet and Higher Education, 7(2), 95-105.

Gilbert, C., & Heller, D. E. (2013). *Community Colleges in the Postwar Era: A Historical Perspective on Innovation and Change.* New Directions for Community Colleges, 2013(162), 7-16.

Gleazer, E. J. (1986). Community Colleges and Federal Policy. *AACC Publications.*

Goldrick-Rab, S. (2010). Challenges and opportunities for improving community college student success. *Review of Educational Research, 80*(3), 437-469.

Goldrick-Rab, S. (2016). Paying the Price: College Costs, Financial Aid, and the Betrayal of the American Dream. Chicago: University of Chicago Press.

Gonzalez, L. (2020). "The Digital Divide and Its Impact on Community Colleges." Community College Journal, 90(3), 14-18.

Gordon, V. N., Habley, W. R., & Grites, T. J. (2008). Academic Advising: A Comprehensive Handbook. San Francisco: Jossey-Bass.

Green, L. (2018). *Maintaining Professionalism in Family-Owned Businesses.* Business Ethics Quarterly.

Grove, A. (2023, April 5). Open admissions at colleges and universities. ThoughtCo. Retrieved from https://www.thoughtco.com/open-admissions-policy-788432

Grubb, W. N., & Gabriner, R. S. (2013). *Basic Skills Education in Community Colleges: Inside and Outside of Classrooms.* Routledge.

Handel, S. J. (2013). The transfer moment: The pivotal partnership between community colleges and four-year institutions in securing the nation's college completion agenda. *New Directions for Higher Education, 2013*(162), 5-15.

Higher Education. (2006). *Prestige or education: college teaching and rigor of courses in prestigious and non-prestigious institutions in the U.S..* Retrieved from https://link.springer.com/article/10.1007/s10734-006-9053-5

Hilton, J. (2016). "Open Educational Resources and College Textbook Choices: A Review of Research on Efficacy and Perceptions." Educational Technology Research and Development, 64(4), 573-590.

Huddleston, J. (2000). A History of the Community College Movement. *Journal of Higher Education.*

Inside Higher Ed. (2023). N.C. legislators gain more power over community colleges. Retrieved from https://www.insidehighered.com/news/2023/09/25/nc-legislators-gain-more-power-over-community-colleges

Jenkins, D., & Fink, J. (2015). *What we know about transfer.* Community College Research Center, Teachers College, Columbia University.

Jenkins, D. (2015). "Redesigning Community Colleges for Student Success." Community College Research Center, Teachers College, Columbia University.

Jenkins, D., & Kerrigan, M. R. (2008). "Evidence-Based Decision Making in Community Colleges: Findings from a Survey of Faculty and Administrator Data Use at Achieving the Dream Colleges." Community College Research Center, Columbia University.

Johnson, M. (2017). *Diversity and Innovation: Challenges in Close-Knit Leadership.* Harvard Business Review.

Johnson, M. (2018). *Effective Communication in Academic Leadership.* Higher Education Quarterly.

Johnson, M. (2020). *Economic impact of COVID-19 on community college students.* Economic Education Review, 29(2), 301-317.

Johnson, L., & Lee, K. (2020). *Resource allocation in higher education.* Higher Education Policy, 28(4), 341-358.

Miller, D. (2016). *Diversity and Inclusion in Academic Leadership.* Journal of Higher Education.

Miller, S. (2022). *The impact of nepotism on public perception in education.* Educational Management Journal, 39(3), 204-218.

Johnstone, S. M., & Soares, L. (2014). "Principles for Developing Competency-Based Education Programs." Change: The Magazine of Higher Learning, 46(2), 12-19.

Jones, A. (2020). *Bias and Favoritism in Workplace Dynamics.* Management Today.

Jones, S. (2019). *Community Colleges and Local Economic Development: A Study of Workforce Training Programs.* Journal of Higher Education Policy and Management, 41(3), 239-256.

Kahneman, D., & Tversky, A. (1979). *Prospect theory: An analysis of decision under risk.* Econometrica, 47(2), 263-292.

Kane, T. J., & Rouse, C. E. (1999). The community college: Educating students at the margin between college and work. *Journal of Economic Perspectives, 13*(1), 63-84.

Karp, M. M. (2011). "Toward a New Understanding of Non-Academic Student Support: Four Mechanisms Encouraging Positive

Student Outcomes in the Community College." Community College Research Center Working Paper No. 28.

Karp, M. M. (2012). *"I don't know, I've never been to college!": Dual Enrollment as a College Readiness Strategy.* New Directions for Higher Education, 158, 21-28.

Katsinas, S. G., Tollefson, T. A., & Reamey, B. A. (2008). Funding and Access Issues in Public Higher Education: A Community College Perspective. New York: Palgrave Macmillan.

Kisker, C. B., & Carducci, R. (2003). "Community College Partnerships with the Private Sector—Organizational Contexts and Models for Successful Collaboration." New Directions for Community Colleges, 2003(123), 21-33.

Kuh, G. D., Kinzie, J., Schuh, J. H., & Whitt, E. J. (2010). Student Success in College: Creating Conditions that Matter. San Francisco: Jossey-Bass.

Kuh, G. D., Kinzie, J., Buckley, J. A., Bridges, B. K., & Hayek, J. C. (2006). What Matters to Student Success: A Review of the Literature. Washington, DC: National Postsecondary Education Cooperative.

Lee, R. (2015). *Risk Management Strategies in Higher Education.* University Administration Journal.

Lewis, K. (2012). *Balancing Personal and Professional Roles in Business.* Entrepreneurial Review.

Levin, J. S. (2001). *Globalizing the Community College: Strategies for Change in the Twenty-First Century.* Palgrave Macmillan.

Levin, J. S., Kater, S. T., & Wagoner, R. L. (2006). *Community College Faculty: At Work in the New Economy.* Palgrave Macmillan.

Levine, A. (2005). Educating school leaders. The Education Schools Project. Retrieved from http://edschools.org/pdf/Final313.pdf.

Ma, J., & Baum, S. (2016). Trends in community colleges: Enrollment, prices, student debt, and completion. *College Board Research.*

Markkula Center for Applied Ethics. (2024). Leadership ethics cases. *Santa Clara University.* Accessed July 18, 2024. Retrieved from https://www.scu.edu/ethics/focus-areas/leadership-ethics/resources/leadership-ethics-cases/

McKay, H., & Devlin, M. (2016). "'Low Cost' and 'High Quality' Higher Education: Catch 22 or Viable Possibility?" European Journal of Education, 51(2), 143-157.

Means, B., Bakia, M., & Murphy, R. (2014). Learning Online: What Research Tells Us About Whether, When and How. New York: Routledge.

Mitchell, J. (2021). *The debt trap: How student loans became a national catastrophe.* Simon & Schuster.

Miller, D. (2013). *Groupthink and Decision-Making in Familiar Environments.* Journal of Management Studies.

Miller, D. (2020). *Balancing home and school: The new normal for community college students.* Higher Education Journal, 38(1), 112-128.

Mintzberg, H. (1994). *The rise and fall of strategic planning.* New York, NY: Free Press.

Monaghan, D. B., & Attewell, P. (2015). The community college route to the bachelor's degree. *Educational Evaluation and Policy Analysis, 37*(1), 70-91.

Montag, M. (1951). Nursing Education and Community Colleges. *Journal of Nursing Education.*

National Center for Education Statistics. (2023). Digest of Education Statistics, 2022. U.S. Department of Education, Institute of Education Sciences. Retrieved from https://nces.ed.gov/programs/digest/

National Center for Education Statistics. (2020, May). *Undergraduate enrollment.* Retrieved from https://nces.ed.gov/programs/coe/indicator_cha.asp

National Student Clearinghouse Research Center. (2020). Transfer and Mobility: A National View of Student Movement in Postsecondary Institutions, Fall 2014 Cohort. Retrieved from https://nscresearchcenter.org/transfer-mobility-report-2020

New America. (2023). Why community college bachelor's degrees? *New America.* Retrieved from [URL]

Niles, S. G., & Harris-Bowlsbey, J. (2013). Career Development Interventions in the 21st Century. Upper Saddle River, NJ: Pearson.

Nuissl, E., & Pehl, K. (2004). "Adult Education and Lifelong Learning in Europe and Beyond." UNESCO Institute for Education.

OECD. (2015). "Students, Computers and Learning: Making the Connection." OECD Publishing.

Osguthorpe, R. T., & Wong, M. J. (1993). The Ph.D. versus the Ed.D.: Time for a decision. *Innovative Higher Education, 18*(1), 47-63.

Pascarella, E. T., & Terenzini, P. T. (2005). How College Affects Students: A Third Decade of Research. San Francisco: Jossey-Bass.

Perna, L. W. (2005). "The Benefits of Higher Education: Sex, Racial/Ethnic, and Socioeconomic Group Differences." Review of Higher Education, 29(1), 23-52.

Perry, J. A. (2016). The Carnegie Project on the Education Doctorate: A Report on the First Year of the Redesign Phase. *Journal of Faculty Development, 30*(2), 65-73.

Pleasants, L. T. (1975). Vocational Education in Community Colleges. *Midwest Educational Review.*

Porter, M. E. (1980). *Competitive strategy: Techniques for analyzing industries and competitors.* New York, NY: Free Press.

Quality Matters. (2019). *Academic rigor: A comprehensive definition.* Retrieved from https://www.qualitymatters.org/sites/default/files/research-docs-pdfs/QM-WP-1-Academic-Rigor-A-Comprehensive-Definition-2019.pdf

Ran, F. X., & Lin, Y. (2019). The effects of corequisite remediation: Evidence from a statewide reform in Tennessee. Educational Evaluation and Policy Analysis, 41(3), 294-317. https://journals.sagepub.com/doi/abs/10.3102/0162373719846024

Renick, T. (2019). "The Unlikely Heroes of Student Success." The Chronicle of Higher Education. Retrieved from https://www.chronicle.com/article/The-Unlikely-Heroes-of/247008

Riggs, J. W. (1985). The Junior College Movement. *American Association of Community Colleges Journal.*

Rowe, D. C., Lunt, B. M., & Ekstrom, J. J. (2011). The role of cyber-security in information technology education. *ACM Transactions on Computing Education (TOCE),* 11(3), 1-15. https://doi.org/10.1145/2037276.2037285

Rumelt, R. P. (2011). *Good strategy bad strategy: The difference and why it matters.* New York, NY: Crown Business.

Russell, J. S. (2024). Leadership development by failure: A case study. *Continuing Studies.* Accessed July 18, 2024. Retrieved from https://continuingstudies.wisc.edu

Santiago, D. A. (2018). *Ensuring Equity in Higher Education: The Role of Community Colleges.* Excelencia in Education.

Schultz, R. E. (1990). Integrating Technical Education into Community Colleges. *Technical Education Review.*

Scrivener, S., Weiss, M. J., Ratledge, A., Rudd, T., Sommo, C., & Fresques, H. (2015). "Doubling Graduation Rates: Three-Year

Effects of CUNY's Accelerated Study in Associate Programs (ASAP) for Developmental Education Students." MDRC.

Selingo, J. J. (2016). There Is Life After College: What Parents and Students Should Know About Navigating School to Prepare for the Jobs of Tomorrow. New York: HarperCollins.

Shulman, L. S., Golde, C. M., Bueschel, A. C., & Garabedian, K. J. (2006). Reclaiming education's doctorates: A critique and a proposal. *Educational Researcher, 35*(3), 25-32.

Smith, J. (2019). *Conflict of Interest in Family Business Leadership.* International Journal of Business Management.

Smith, J. (2019). *Hiring practices in community colleges: An ethical perspective.* Ethics in Education, 17(1), 56-67.

Smith, A. A. (2010). "Enrollment Trends in Higher Education: A Look at Community Colleges." Journal of Higher Education Policy and Management, 32(1), 25-38.

Smith, A. A. (2020). *The Digital Transformation of Community Colleges: Enhancing Learning and Accessibility.* EDUCAUSE Review.

Smith, J. (2020). *Institutional Policies and Best Practices.* Academic Management Review.

Smith, J. (2021). *The digital divide and its impact on remote learning.* Technology in Education Quarterly, 44(2), 198-214.

Smith, J., & Abou-Sayf, F. K. (2006). *Professional development: A guide to resources.* Community College Press.

Soares, L. (2013). "Postsecondary Education and Training as We Know It Is Not Enough: Why We Need to Leverage Competency-Based Education to Rapidly Re-Employ Americans." Center for American Progress.

State Higher Education Executive Officers Association (SHEEO). (2018). State Higher Education Finance Report. Retrieved from https://sheeo.org/project/state-higher-education-finance

Taylor, P. (2016). *Employee Motivation and Perceived Fairness.* Human Resource Management Journal.

Taylor, P. (2019). *Performance Improvement in Higher Education Leadership.* Human Resource Management Journal.

Taylor, P. (2020). *Institutional support and student retention during COVID-19.* Community College Journal, 33(3), 174-190.

Taylor, S., & Rege, A. (2020). Cybersecurity and community colleges: The emerging role of cybersecurity education in two-year institutions. *Community College Journal of Research and Practice,* 44(1), 17-31. https://doi.org/10.1080/10668926.2018.1556134

Tierney, W. G. (1997). *Academic outlaws: Queer theory and cultural studies in the academy.* Sage Publications.

The Edvocate. (2018). Why all community colleges should offer bachelor's degrees. *The Edvocate.* Retrieved from [URL]

Thelin, J. R. (2011). A History of American Higher Education. Baltimore: Johns Hopkins University Press.

Tinto, V. (2003). "Learning Better Together: The Impact of Learning Communities on Student Success." Higher Education Monograph Series, 2003-1. Syracuse University.

Tinto, V. (2012). Completing College: Rethinking Institutional Action. Chicago: University of Chicago Press.

Thompson, P. (2021). *Governance and accountability in higher education institutions.* Journal of Educational Governance, 23(2), 99-115.

Townsend, B. K., & Twombly, S. B. (2007). *Community College Faculty: Overlooked and Undervalued.* ASHE Higher Education Report, Volume 32, Number 6. John Wiley & Sons.

University of California. (n.d.). Transfer credit. Retrieved from https://admission.universityofcalifornia.edu/admission-requirements/transfer-requirements/transfer-credit.html

Upcraft, M. L., Gardner, J. N., & Barefoot, B. O. (2005). Challenging and Supporting the First-Year Student: A Handbook for Improving the First Year of College. San Francisco: Jossey-Bass.

U.S. Bureau of Labor Statistics. (2024). *Measuring the value of education: Career Outlook.* Retrieved from BLS.

U.S. Department of Education, National Center for Education Statistics (NCES). (2019). The Condition of Education 2019 (NCES 2019-144), Undergraduate Retention and Graduation Rates. Retrieved from https://nces.ed.gov/programs/coe/indicator_ctr.asp

U.S. Department of Education. (2020). *The Benefits of Higher Education.* Retrieved from Ed.gov

Williams, B. (2014). *Succession Planning and Leadership Development in Family Firms.* Strategic Management Journal.

Williams, B. (2017). *Financial Management for Academic Leaders.* Strategic Management Journal.

Williams, B. (2020). *Academic challenges and remote learning during the pandemic.* Journal of Online Learning, 27(4), 403-419.

Xu, D., & Jaggars, S. S. (2013). The impact of online learning on students' course outcomes: Evidence from a large community and technical college system. *Economics of Education Review*, 37, 46-57. https://doi.org/10.1016/j.econedurev.2013.08.001

About the Author

Douglas B. Sims, PhD, is an accomplished environmental soil scientist with over three decades of experience, including more than 20 years in the environmental consulting industry, where he built and led successful companies across the nation. In 2011, he transitioned to higher education, bringing his extensive expertise to academia. Over the past 14 years, Dr. Sims has dedicated himself to advancing student success and workforce development, initially as an environmental science instructor and later as the Dean of the School of Science, Engineering, and Mathematics at a leading community college.

Dr. Sims is widely published in peer-reviewed journals, contributing valuable research to his field. Beyond his professional accomplishments, he is deeply interested in human behavior, corporate dynamics, management, and leadership strategies. Married to his college sweetheart since the early 1990s, Dr. Sims and his wife have raised two grown children. Drawing on his unique blend of experience in industry and academia, Dr. Sims combines scientific expertise with a profound curiosity about leadership and organizational growth, offering a distinctive perspective that bridges both worlds.